NECTAR FROM HEAVEN

STORIES FROM HEART TO HEART

ALBERT LOW

Illustrations by
Jean Austin Low
And Jeffrey Frith

Monk: Who can bring the nectar of heaven?

Zen master Joshu: Thank you for bringing it to me.

Introduction

I have used the stories and inspirational pieces in this collection during talks that I have given over many years spent as a Zen teacher. Each story has a point to make that would be difficult to spell out in specific detail, but which has the potential to change the way we see the world. Stories and inspirational texts have always been used in this way. To see what I mean, one only has to think of the parables of Jesus, the fables of Lafontaine and Aesop, the stories about the exploits of Mullah Nassr Eddin, the stories of Jalaluddin Rumi, and the famous Mahabharata of which the Bhagavad Gita forms a part.

Much of the therapy that the hypnotherapist, Milt Erikson, gave was delivered in the form of stories. Stories by-pass the 'conscious' mind, and directly influence the 'unconscious.' Jokes, poetry, and listening to the words spoken from beyond the conscious mind of the speaker, also do this.

Most of us are now quite used to using the words 'conscious' and 'unconscious' mind, but few of us are sure what the words mean. Indeed, the very idea of an 'unconscious' mind, or an 'unconscious consciousness,' seems to be a contradiction in terms. The word 'unconscious' generally means lacking awareness and the ability to see, hear, feel or think.

Freud popularized the term, and we owe much of our understanding of the 'unconscious' to him. Freud understood the word to mean some kind of container or reservoir of feelings, thoughts, urges, and memories that lies below our conscious awareness. Because these unconscious contents are painful and conflicting, Freud said, they are suppressed. He taught that the unconscious has a continuous influence on our lives, and modifies much of our behavior. But, if we not at some level aware of this influence, how can it affect us?

The Freudian use of the word 'unconscious,' implies in some way 'less than conscious,' or 'inferior' to conscious, and this is unfortunate. The unconscious is believed, by some people, to provide much of the motivation for action, and is even given creative powers, and this rather contradicts the idea of an inferior mind.

Again, Freud was partly responsible for this misunderstanding. An aim of his therapy was to make the 'unconscious conscious.' He said something to the effect of "Where there is Id [the unconscious] let there be ego." The implication of this approach is that the conscious mind is the superior mind.

But Eastern thought generally, and Buddhist thought specifically, tends to think otherwise, and believes that the 'unconscious' mind is the superior mind. Recent psychological research seems to support this. By exploring this alternative way of seeing the workings of our mind, we can see more clearly how stories acquire their power to influence us.

We have two minds, or two ways in which we are aware: we are aware *as* the world, and aware *of* the world. As you sit reading this book, you are aware *as* the book, and you are aware *of* aspects of the book. You are aware *as* the page and the print, and you are aware *of* what the book is saying. You are also aware *as* the room and the surroundings. Awareness *of* is generally seen as the conscious mind, and awareness *as* is seen as 'the unconscious,' although, as can readily be seen, neither mind is unaware.

The following examples will help you to see what I mean by 'awareness of' being the conscious, and 'awareness as' being the unconscious.

You were aware *as* the period at the end of the last sentence. As soon as I say this you become aware *of* it. That you were aware *as* it is evident because it modified the way you read the sentence. Yet, until I drew your attention to it, the presence of the period escaped you. You are aware *as* the pressure of the seat against your legs; as soon as I say this you become aware *of* it. The expression 'aware *as*' is used very deliberately because *what* 'you are aware as,' and 'your awareness,' are not two; they are not the same, but they not separate. This could also be said of a mirror and its reflections: they are not the same, but they cannot be separated.

To understand a little further the use of the word 'as' in the expression awareness *as*, consider these two sentences: the man appeared *as* Father Christmas; the man appeared *to be* Father Christmas. The man, in the first sentence, is, or cannot be separated from, the role of Father Christmas; in the second sentence he is separate from Father Christmas.

Awareness *of* is sometimes referred to as the 'discriminating mind.' It is the mind we use when we focus on particular aspects of our experience: when we pick out the face of a friend in a crowd, when we choose an apple in the supermarket, when we study the menu at a restaurant. It is the mind that we use when we add up a column of figures, analyze a problem, or compare two alternative courses of action.

A child psychologist, Alison Gopnik, in her researches into infant development has suggested that the child's mind operates in a different way to the way that the mind of an adult works. In this she gives some experimental support to our having two minds. The way a child's mind operates, she says, is in a diffuse, non-directed way; an adult's mind, on the other hand, is directed and focused. The first she calls *lantern* awareness; the second *spotlight* awareness.

Suppose you have to find something in the basement, which is quite dark. You can either: take a spotlight and shine it around; or you can turn on the basement light. In the first instance the light picks out individual objects, in the second everything is lit up equally. As we can see, lantern awareness corresponds to some extent to awareness as; spotlight awareness corresponds to awareness of.

Lantern awareness, or awareness as, is the creative awareness: it is the awareness with which we read a novel or see a movie, the mind with which we dream. Research into creativity has shown that there is an incubation period during which the problem one is working on sinks into the 'unconscious.' It is well known that if one has a particularly difficult problem then one should 'sleep on it.' This 'unconscious' out of which creative solutions emerge is the lantern mind.

Whereas lantern awareness is open to all experience, spotlight awareness is discriminating and selective, it analyzes and divides; it is concerned with elements and objects. Lantern awareness is interested in relations and meanings; spotlight awareness rejects and acts as a filter on experience. Thus lantern awareness gives much richer, closer to life, experience than spotlight awareness. Spotlight awareness, on the other hand, gives us control, and enables us to make changes and improvements; it is the instrument of science and mathematics, of logic and philosophy.

When we read or listen to a story, or when we are inspired by something we are told, we use awareness *as*, and we live, or 'inhabit,' the story. We 'become,' so to speak, the characters. A well-written story provides us with essential clues to make this possible. We need a certain amount of character description, of information about the environment, the time of the year and the time of day. A good writer is able to do this with the minimum of words. We, as readers, must clothe these words with feelings, with perceptions, judgments and with action. By living the story we are affected by it. This is why, at the beginning of this introduction, I said that each story has a point to make that would be difficult to spell out in specific detail, but which has the potential to change the way we see the world.

When you read this book therefore, let what you read dwell in the mind. I have added a short verse or sometimes an aphorism to each story. Some of these additions amplify the theme of the story; others simply embellish it. Do not be in a hurry to get on to the next story. Indeed, this could be a very good bedtime book that you read just before retiring for the night. What you read could then stay with that mind beyond consciousness. I have deliberately avoided giving 'explanations' of what the story means or implies. To do so would be to forestall the reader's lantern mind and take away the value of the story

A little boy
goes to heaven

A little boy knocked on the gates of heaven, and, when St. Peter came to him, asked to be allowed in. St. Peter told the boy to wait while he consulted with God. While he waited the boy looked around at the vast and wide landscape that surrounded him. The season being late autumn, the trees were covered with leaves: gold, crimson, orange and green. As far as the eye could see blazed trees upon trees, hills upon hills, of flaming beauty.

St. Peter returned. "I have God's answer. Do you see all of those trees?" and he swept his hand around the full 360 degree of the horizon. The little boy replied, "Yes." Peter went on, "God said that when the leaves have fallen from all those trees as many times as there are leaves on the trees, you may come into heaven."

The little boy sat down without haste and, looking up at St. Peter, said, "Please tell God the first leaf has fallen."

Time and time again.

Have the mountains turned from green to gold –
Fickle earth!
Dust in your eyes, the triple world is too narrow;
With nothing in the mind, your sitting-cushion is wide enough.
Muso

The Rabbi's distress

A true story is told about a rabbi whose custom it was to hear, one by one, the confessions and problems of his disciples. The disciples would go into the rabbi's room for the interview. When they left the room they would leave the door ajar, signaling the next in line that the rabbi was free.

During one such time, a chief disciple noticed that the rabbi's door had been closed for quite a long while, and the waiting room was full of anxious disciples. Finally, he could wait no longer and, contrary to custom, gently pushed the door open to see what was going on.

To his amazement he found the rabbi sitting with his head buried in his hands. The chief disciple asked what the matter was and, in reply, the rabbi simply leapt up and demanded the community declare a fast for him, and to assemble for afternoon prayer.

Later, two disciples asked him about what had happened. The rabbi answered that when he listened to people's problems, sins, and worries, he looked inside himself to find a similar disposition to what his disciple was saying. The last disciple he listened to had told such a terrible story that the rabbi could find nothing in his own life to match it. "I was struck down by this," said the rabbi, "because it could only mean that such a similarity did exist, but I had felt the need to suppress it in myself."

There is no better method of approaching this Word than in silence, in quiet; we hear it aright in unknowing. To one who knows naught, it is clearly revealed.

The enchanted frog

Once upon a time there lived a merchant who had three daughters, but his wife died while the children were still young. He made up his mind to travel across the sea to find gold and jewels. His children wept in distress at the idea of their father leaving them, but he comforted them by saying, "I will bring each of you a gift. Tell me, what you would like above all?"

The oldest daughter begged him to bring her a beautiful silk dress, made of three kinds of silk.

The second asked for a hat with three kinds of feathers.

The youngest finally said, "Bring me a rose; but it must be fresh and have three colors."

The merchant promised to bring them their gifts, bade them goodbye, and left.

Arriving in the foreign land, he bought the dress with three kinds of silk for his oldest daughter, and the hat with three kinds of feathers for the second daughter. Both dress and hat were very beautiful. Then, for his youngest daughter—the one he loved the most— he had messengers travel across the whole country, looking for a rose with three colors. He promised to pay the highest price. Even though roses were plentiful in that land, the messengers could not find a rose with three colors, and they returned empty handed.

Downcast, with a very heavy heart, the merchant returned to his home country. Arriving there, he came across a garden filled with roses. He entered the garden to look around. His eyes immediately fell on a small bush in the center of the garden. Growing from the bush was a rose with three colors.

Overjoyed, he plucked the rose, and was about to leave the garden with it when he was, by magic, frozen in place. He then heard a voice coming from behind demanding, "What are you doing in my garden?" Startled, he looked around and saw a big frog sitting by a garden pond, staring at him with wide eyes. The frog went on to say, "Look what you have done to my rose! I prized it above all. You must let me marry your youngest daughter, otherwise you forfeit your life." The merchant was terrified. He begged the frog to ask for something else; he would agree to any other

But the frog was adamant. In the end the merchant had to agree to the frog marrying his daughter. Immediately, his feet became unfrozen, and he could leave the garden without difficulty. As he left, the frog said,"I shall come for my wife in seven days."

With a heavy heart the merchant gave the daughter the fresh rose with three colors, and explained to her what had happened. When the dreaded day arrived, she hid in a closet because she was afraid, and did not even want to see the frog. og reminded him. wish.

At noon, a magnificent carriage arrived. The frog ordered his servants to search for the young girl. They searched the house, under the bed, and into all the closets. At last, they found the hidden daughter, and dragging her from her hiding place, carried her, screaming, into the carriage.

The driver whipped the horses into action, and, in a short while they arrived in the beautiful rose garden. At the center of the garden, by the pond, stood a small house. The servants took the young bride into the house, and laid her on a soft bed. In the meantime the frog, leapt into the water.

Darkness fell, and after sleeping for a while, the maiden woke up to hear the frog outside her window, singing beautiful and tender songs. As midnight approached, he sang ever more sweetly, and, coming into the house slowly approached her room. At midnight exactly, the bedroom door opened, and the frog jumped onto her bed.

However, he had touched her heart with his gentle singing, and she allowed him into her bed, covering him up, and embracing him warmly.

The next morning, as she opened her eyes, she found to her astonishment that the frog had become a handsome prince. He thanked her, with all his heart, saying, "Your love has saved me from the spell. Now you are really my wife!" And they lived happily ever after.

If you knew how to suffer,
You would have the power not to suffer.
Hymn of Jesus.

Faith

Therefore, Subhuti, all Bodhisattvas should arouse a pure, clear, non-reflecting mind that is not dependent upon seeing, hearing, tasting, smelling, touching or any quality at all. A Bodhisattva should arouse the mind without resting it upon anything.

Diamond Sutra

Master: Think the unthinkable!

Monk: How do you do that?"

Master: Without ideas, images, thoughts or concepts.

The Trappist's Dilemma[1]

The Trappist order had a rule of absolute silence. Monks could communicate by signs, but these should only be used in exceptional cases.

A Trappist Father tells the following true story: he became very troubled because the brother next to him in choir kept prostrating himself. Prostrating was called 'knuckling,' and one would knuckle to express humility, or to ask God's forgiveness for some imperfection or sin. It was called knuckling because one would prostrate on all fours, with the knuckles of one's hand on the floor, and the head by the knees

This brother kept knuckling, and the Father in question began to think that these prostrations occurred because of something he, the Father, was doing—or else something about him was bothering the priest who was knuckling. They would be singing or chanting, and all of a sudden, the brother would knuckle. The priest wondered whether there was something wrong with him: was he singing off key, or perhaps he had body odor, or the smell of his breath was bad?

The priest became increasingly certain that he was the cause of the brother's constant knuckling, He felt that he must be doing something the brother resented, and then became guilty about his resentment.

This doubt gnawed away at the priest for at least six months. It even seemed a lot longer than it was, because in those days the monks were spending whole days in the choir, and he had no one with whom he could discuss the problem.

Finally, he made up his mind that he had had enough and was determined to get to the bottom of the whole affair. So, he decided to speak to the Father Superior about the matter. He did so, and asked the Father Superior to find out what it was that he was doing that so disturbed the brother.

In a few days the Father Superior called him into the office with the answer. He told the priest, "He does not know that you exist."

What then do we experience of you?
Just nothing. For we do not experience it.
What then do we know of you?
Everything. For we know nothing isolated
anymore.

Martin Buber

But often, in the din of strife,
There rises an unspeakable desire
After the knowledge of our buried life;
A thirst to spend our fire and restless force
In tracking out our true, original course;
A longing to inquire
Into the mystery of this heart which beats
So wild, so deep in us — to know
Whence our lives come and where they go.
And many a man in his own breast then delves,
But deep enough, alas! no-one ever mines.
And we have been on many thousand lines,
And we have shown, on each, spirit and power;
But hardly have we, for one little hour,
Been on our own line, have we been ourselves —
Hardly had skill to utter one of all
The nameless feelings that course through our breast,
But they course on forever unexpress'd.
And long we try in vain to speak and act
Our hidden self, and what we say and do
Is eloquent, is well — but 't is not true!
And then we will no more be rack'd
With inward striving, and demand
Of all the thousand nothings of the hour
Their stupefying power;
Ah yes, and they benumb us at our call!

Yet still, from time to time, vague and forlorn,
From the soul's subterranean depth upborne
As from an infinitely distant land,
Come airs, and floating echoes, and convey
A melancholy into all our day.

Mathew Arnold

This earth where we stand is the pure Lotus Land
And this very body, the body of Buddha.
Hakuin.

Travellers on the road

An old man used to sit by the roadside and greet travelers as they passed. On one occasion, he asked a traveler, "Where do you come from?" "From back there, that last town on the road," replied the traveler. "What was it like?" asked the old man. "Terrible," said the traveler. "The people were unfriendly, there were no jobs, and the place was quite ugly." "Where are you going to?" "To the next town down the road." "I know it quite well," said the old man. "What is it like?" asked the traveler. "Terrible," replied the old man, "the people are unfriendly, there are hardly any jobs and it is quite an ugly town." The traveler went on his despondent way.

On another occasion the old man asked another traveler, "Where do you come from?" "From back there, that last town on the road," replied the traveler. "What was it like?" asked the old man. "Wonderful," said the traveler. "The people were very friendly, there were plenty of jobs, and the place was quite beautiful." "Where are you going to?" "To the next town down the road." "I know it quite well," said the old man. "What is it like?" asked the traveler. "Wonderful," replied the old man, "the people are very friendly, there is plenty of work, and it is quite a beautiful town."

Coming and going we never leave home

Hakuin

Life is suffering

A woman went to Buddha with her baby in her arms. The baby was dead; a snake had bitten it. She begged Buddha to help her, to give her some relief from her suffering. Buddha said, "Yes, I can do that; but first you must bring me a mustard seed. It must come from a house that has not known suffering." She left on her quest for the mustard seed. After a while she came back to Buddha and said, "I can find many mustard seeds, but I cannot find a seed that comes from a house that has not known suffering."

Buddha said,
My sister, thou hast found,
Searching for what none finds, that bitter balm
I had to give thee. He thou lovest slept
Dead on thy bosom yesterday; today
Thou knowest the whole wide world weeps with thy
woe.

Who then devised the torment? Love.
Love is the unfamiliar Name
Behind the hands that wove
The intolerable shirt of flame
Which human power cannot remove.

T.S.Eliot

Not knowing

A scholar who lived in Mullah Nasr Eddin's village would go around boasting, "I know," "I know." One day, Mullah in turn, went around the village saying, "I don't know, I don't know." A friend was concerned about Mullah, and asked him, "Mullah, why do you go around bragging about your ignorance?" Mullah replied, "Everyone knows they know; not knowing they know is rare."

I know not who I am,
but what I know I'm not:
a thing - yet a no-thing
a circle - yet a center.

Angelus Sileseus

Lighting a fire.

Zen practice is something like this: Suppose you are out camping and want to light a fire for warmth, and to cook by. You have just one match, it has rained just a while ago and the ground is still damp. What will you do?

First, you would light a few leaves, dry ones. Then you gather a few more and gently add these to the flame...then a few more. Perhaps now a twig or two, and more leaves. More twigs now and a few small branches. Careful!! a few more smaller branches can be added to what is now a small blaze. Now, some bigger branches. Not too big! Now some more, and more. Now, those bigger branches, soon a roaring fire throws its heat and light around the camp. If you wanted to you could now set whole trees on the fire: even burn down the forest itself.

Why does it rain on the sea?

Mind is like vast space

Mind is like vast space in which there is no confusion or evil, as when the sun wheels through it shining upon the four corners of the world. For, when the sun rises and illumines the whole earth, space gains not in brilliance; and, when the sun sets, space does not darken. The phenomena of light and darkness alternate with each other, but the nature of the void remains unchanged.

So it is with the Mind of the Buddha and of sentient beings. If you look upon the Buddha as presenting a pure, bright or Awakened appearance, or upon sentient beings as presenting a foul, dark or mortal seeming appearance, these conceptions resulting from attachment to form will keep you from supreme knowing, even after the passing of as many eons as there

There is only the One Mind and not a particle of anything else on which to lay hold, for this Mind is the Buddha. If you students of the Way do not awaken to the reality of Mind you will overlay Mind with conceptual thought, you will seek the Buddha outside yourselves, and you will remain attached to forms, pious practices and so on, all of which are harmful and not at all the way to supreme knowing.

Zen master Huang Po

The Lord is in my eye.
That is why I see him everywhere.

Death, where is thy sting?

A monk declared, "Buddhism says that truth is eternal. In what way should we apply our minds?" Joshu said, "Listen, the emperors Zenkan and Gokan ruled all of China but at the moment of death they could not even make use of a cent."

***

It is not death that is the source of all man's evils, and of a mean and cowardly spirit: but rather the fear of death. Epictetus

***

There is no death of any one but in the appearance, even as there is no birth of any save in the seeming. The change from being to becoming seems to be birth, and the change from becoming to being seems to be death, but in reality no one is ever born, nor does anyone ever die.

Apollonius of Tyana

***

If there's death, then what am I? If I am, then what is death?

***

He was a patient in the terminal patients ward of a large hospital in Montreal. He said to me, "You know, I have just one wish." "What is your wish?" I asked. "That I had another six weeks to live." He was dead in a few days.

***

You, young fellow, if you don't want to die, die now. Once dead, you don't have to die twice. Hakuin.

***

"All life is noumenal only…the whole world of sense is only a picture hovering before us, formed by our present mode of knowledge—a dream lacking any objective reality in itself." Emmanuel Kant.

***

At the funeral of one of his monks Joshu remarked, "What a long procession of dead bodies following the wake of one living person!"

"To be a living being is not the ultimate; there is something beyond, much more marvelous and wonderful than existence or non-existence, life or death. It is the state of pure presence, which transcends space and time. Once we let go of the illusion that the body mind is all there is, death loses its terrifying face, it becomes one with life."

Nisargadatta

Life in death

(The following was taken from a letter written by a young Canadian seaman to his mother. He was sentenced to death by The Nazis had sentenced him to death for smuggling arms into France.)

I know that you are a courageous woman and that you will be able to bear this proof of your faith. But, listen to me, it is not enough that you bear it; you must understand it.

I am an insignificant thing, and my person will soon be forgotten, but the thought, the life, the inspiration that filled me will live on. You will meet them every-where — in the trees at springtime, in people who you meet on the way, in a loving little smile. You will encounter that something that perhaps had value in me, you will cherish it, and you will not forget me. And I will have a chance to grow, to become large and mature. I shall be living with you whose hearts I once filled And you will live on, knowing that I have pre-ceded you, and not as perhaps you might have thought at first, dropped out behind you."

Death be not proud

Death be not proud, though some have called thee

Mighty and dreadfull, for, thou art not so,

For, those, whom thou think'st, thou dost overthrow,

Die not, poore death, nor yet canst thou kill me.

From rest and sleepe, which but thy pictures bee,

Much pleasure, then from thee, much more must flow,

And soonest our best men with thee doe goe,

Rest of their bones, and soules deliverie.

Thou art slave to Fate, Chance, kings, and desperate
men,

And dost with poyson, warre, and sicknesse dwell,

And poppie, or charmes can make us sleepe as well,

And better then thy stroake; why swell'st thou then;

One short sleepe past, wee wake eternally,

And death shall be no more; death, thou shalt die.

John Donne

Do not stand at my grave and weep.
I am not there, I do not sleep.
I am a thousand winds that blow,
I am the diamond glints on snow.
I am the sunlight on ripened grain,
I am the gentle autumn's rain.
When you awaken in the morning's hush,
I am the swift uplifting rush
of quiet birds in circled flight.
I am the stars that shine at night.
Do not stand at my grave and cry,
I am not there, I did not die . . .

-Anonymous

The monk and
the young woman

Two Buddhist monks were on pilgrimage, and one day while traveling they met a young woman who was obviously deeply distressed. She was blocked from going forward because of a wide stretch of water and mud. She was afraid that if she went forward she would muddy her long robe, and yet she could not stay where she was.

One of the monks, seeing her plight, swept her up in his arms, and strode through the mud and water. Arriving at the other side he set her down, and with his companion, went on his way. After a short while, his companion turned to the monk and said, "What you did back there was quite wrong. You know our order forbids us to touch a woman!" "Are you still carrying that woman? I set her down ten minutes ago," said the monk.

It is not what goes into your mouths that defiles you. It is what comes out of them.

   Jesus

Getting the cow into the barn

Milt Erikson tells this story: His father wanted to get a cow into the barn. He had tied a rope around her neck and was trying to pull her in the direction he wanted her to go. However, the more he pulled, the more the cow dug her feet into the ground and refused to budge. It was obvious to Milt that his father was fighting a losing battle.

Milt called out, "Leave her be for a moment; I'll get her into the barn." His father let go of the rope and Milt grabbed hold of the cow's tail and used it to pull her for all he was worth away from the barn. Again the cow pulled hard but in the opposite direction. Little by little, Milt let her pull him into the barn.

Man has to awaken to wonder;
science is a way of sending him off to sleep again

Wittgenstein

A glass of water

Two figures trudge through the heat and dust. At first black shadows, they emerge from the glare and shimmer of the sun: an old man, bent, weary; a young man alert, solicitous. They come to a tree throwing its shade aslant the track. Some twenty feet beyond the tree, dwells a small cottage slumbering on the banks of a dried out river. The old man sits wearily in the shade. He asks, "Elam, will you please bring me some water from that cottage?" "Yes, yes, I'll be right back," replies Elam.

The young man turns quickly, goes to the house and knocks on the door. After a few minutes, a beautiful young girl opens the door, and somewhat shyly enquires, "Good day, can I help you?"

"My teacher is weary and thirsty. Could you please give me some water for him."

"Of course will you not come in for a moment while I get it for you?"

Elam walks in, and at the girl's invitation, sits down. "Could I get you a drink as well?" She asks.

Elam agrees, and she brings the drink to him. They talk, and to their surprise find they were both born in the same small village, some ten miles away. They search their memories for common experiences: friends shared, places visited, and soon find that they have much in common. Lana, for that was the girl's name, insists that she get something for the young man to eat. Gradually, the afternoon merges with evening, and evening with the dark of night. Elam realizes that he can no longer live without Lana, and Lana, in her turn, looks down and smiles.

One thing led to another and, as is so often the case in these kinds of things, they declared their love for each other, became betrothed, and eventually married.

During the rainy season the dried out river became a fast moving waterway, and, by hard work and by using different kinds of irrigation devices, Elam managed to develop a large area of the land as a garden for growing many different kinds of fruit and vegetables. Lana, too, helped from early morning to late in the evening. They did so well that they were able to supply a good deal of the neighboring villages with fruit and vegetables.

In time they had two babies. First a girl was born and then, just over a year later, a baby boy. Elam, with the help of some neighbors, enlarged the house and made a beautiful garden full of flowers in which the children could play under the watchful eye of Lana.

Their lives prospered, and as the years passed their love grew ever deeper, and they felt sure nothing could ever mar their joy. One year, however, the rainy season was much more severe. It started earlier, and rained harder until soon it flooded down in sheets. The wind blew great, gray clouds, in which the lightning flashed and flickered, and thunder rumbled. Day after day the rain poured down, heavier and heavier, until earth and sky became a single wash of water. The river rose up its banks, flooded over the hard won gardens that became first a marsh, then a lake. But still it rained. The waters inched up the walls of the house.

Elam moved his small family to the second floor.

At first he had not worried very much. The rainy season was always a very wet one. Yet, the waters were rising too fast, and who knows whether the dam that caused the river to dry out each summer would not break. He sat, and looked anxiously at the river hour after hour, day after day, peering through the streaming rain trying to judge from the movement of the water if the dam was still holding. All through the night he sat while Lana slept peacefully and trustingly by his side, cradling the young boy in her arms, her daughter lying but a few short feet away.

Dawn came. The black of night gave way to a gray, sullen, streaming day. As he looked, his eyes worn and sore, a wave rolled down the river, and another then another, bigger one. The dam had burst. "Quickly! quickly!" he cried, "We must get out." But even as the family struggled out of the drug of sleep, and got ready to go down the stairs, Elam saw it was already too late. The water rose steadily, swiftly up the side of the house. The first floor was already lost to the water, which was now greedily lapping its way into the second. He cried out to Lana, "We must get out on to the roof, any minute now it will be too deep in here for the children."

First, Lana forced her way through the narrow window that opened onto the sloping roof, and then Elam passed the two frightened children out after her. Already knee deep in water he followed his small brood out on to the roof, exposed to the biting, rushing wind, pelted by rain. They clung to the peak of the roof shivering, looking across the vast landscape, a water wasteland of terror.

The wind tugged and pulled. Lana clung desperately to her children trying to anchor herself so that she would not slip down the steep slope of the roof. Elam clung to her. All around was nothing but water and debris carried by the water: dead cows, and struggling horses, trees, roofs of houses, carts, all bobbed and jostled their way down the center of this gray, freezing torrent.

Lana turned to Elam. "I'm getting so tired. Will you not hold the boy for a short while to give me a chance to rest?" She reached out to pass the boy to the out-stretched arms of her husband, but, as she did so, she accidentally struck the little girl, who lost her hold and began to slip down the roof. Lana cried out in anguish, and stretched down to catch the little girl, and just caught her dress. But then she too began to slide, and the only way to stop herself would be to let go of her daughter, and this she would not do. Faster and faster, both slid, and Elam put the boy down and managed to put his foot far enough down the roof so that his wife could grab it, and check her fall. Husband, wife and daughter strung out on the wet slippery roof suspend-ed in a time of agony. The boy cried, rolled over and slid down the roof, the father lunged out, dislodged his wife and she plunged down, following her two chil-dren into the swirling waters to be swept along with the rushing flood bearing its strange and demented cargo.

Elam clung to the roof. First he saw a small hand, then his wife's face, then a foot, and then all was gone. The rain lashed down, the water mingling with his tears of grief.

The wind blew and moaned and deep in the depths he heard his teacher say, "Won't you please knock on the door again? I am very thirsty and would like a drink." Elam turned and knocked again, but he knew the house was empty.

Thus shall you think of all this fleeting world
A star at dawn, a bubble in a stream;
A flash of lightning in a summer cloud,
A flickering lamp, a phantom and a dream.

The Diamond Sutra

The goat

A man went to the great Tibetan sage, Milarepa, to ask for his teaching. Milarepa agreed, but said, "First you must collect together all that you own and bring it to me." The man went home, collected together all that he owned, and set off back to Milarepa, taking his possessions with him. Shortly after beginning his return journey, he came across his old, lame goat. Seeing it he wondered whether to take it along with him and give it also to Milarepa. He then thought, "No, the goat is old and lame. Milarepa would not want it," and continued on his way.

When he arrived he gave his belongings to Milarepa, who asked, "Is this all that you have?" "Yes," said the man. Then he remembered the goat. "There was a goat, but he was old and lame, so I left it," he said.

"Go and get the goat!" said Milarepa

Monk: The common people cherish riches. What is it the monk values?
Joshu: Quickly – shut your mouth!
Monk: Will that do if I shut my mouth?
Joshu: If you don't shut your mouth how are you going to get at it?

You're right

The counsel for the prosecution put forward his case. "You're right," said the judge.

The counsel for the defense stated his case. "You're right," said the judge.

"But m'lord," stuttered the clerk of the court, "they both can't be right!"

"You're right," said the judge.

Q. The one who is beyond right and wrong, does hobtain deliverance?
Joshu. He does not.
Q. Why not?
Joshu. Because he is within right and wrong.

The donkey
who would not work

A farmer had a donkey that would not work. The farmer did all that he could to get it to do so, but to no avail. Eventually, in despair, he asked his neighbor for advice. "You must give the donkey plenty of love and compassion," declared the neighbor. "Love and compassion!" exclaimed the farmer. "Yes," said the neighbor. "It works wonders."

The two separated and the farmer returned to his donkey. After a couple of weeks the farmer happened to meet the neighbor. "How is the donkey?" asked the neighbor. "Is he working now?" "Not at all," said the farmer. "What you suggested has made no difference." "Let me see him," said the neighbor, and the two went off to find the donkey in a nearby stall.

As the neighbor approached the donkey he seized a two by four, and, going straight up to the donkey, brought it down on to its head with a sharp crack. "But," stammered the farmer, "but I thought you said one must use love and compassion." "Yes," said the neighbor, "but first you must get its attention."

Q. What is the ultimate teaching of Zen?
Zen Master Issa: Attention! Attention! Attention!

Rinzai

Followers of the way, mind is without form and pervades the ten directions:

In the eye it is called seeing,

In the ear it is called hearing.

In the nose it smells odors,

In the mouth it holds converse.

In the hands it grasps and seizes,

In the feet it runs and carries.

Fundamentally, it is one pure radiance; divided it becomes harmoniously united spheres of sense. Since the mind is non-existent, wherever you go you are free.

Purity of heart is to will one thing
Kierkegaard

The servant
of the king

Mullah was appointed to the court of the king, and he spent some time learning how to behave.

One day the king was very hungry, and it so happened that on that day the chef had cooked some eggplants that were so delicious the king ordered him to serve them every day.

The king asked, "Aren't eggplants the most tasty vegetable in the whole world?"

Mullah replied saying, "Indeed they are!"

The chef, as ordered, continued to serve eggplants each day for a week. Finally, the king had had enough. "Take these things away and get rid of them," he shouted. "Aren't they the worst vegetable in the whole world?"

Mullah agreed, "Indeed they are!"

"But Mullah," asked the King, "didn't you say a week ago that they were the best of all vegetables?"

"Indeed I did. But, then, I am the servant of the King not of eggplants."

Yesterday upon the stair
I met a man who wasn't there
He wasn't there again today
Oh, how I wish he'd go away.

William Hughes Mearns

Compassion

A dove flew over a forest. When it looked down, it saw that the forest was a blazing inferno. Animals and birds rushed around in panic as the fire threatened to engulf them. The dove felt compassion for all the suffering life. It flew on until it came to the ocean. Over the ocean, it dived, and gathering a few drops of water onto its back, flew back to the forest. After arriving, it shook the few drops of water on to the raging flames. Again, it flew to the ocean. Again, it gathered a few drops of water and returned to the fire to sprinkle the water on it. Again and again, it made the wearying journey. Eventually, arriving over the fire, and after dropping a few more drops of water, it was so exhausted that it could go no further.

It plunged to its death into the furnace.

Truly, truly, I say to you, unless a grain of wheat falls into the earth and dies, it remains alone; but if it dies it bears much fruit. The one who loves his life loses it and he who turns aside from life in this world shall keep it for eternal life.

Jesus

To be a Slave
of Intensity

Friend, hope for the guest while you are alive.

Jump into experience while you are alive!

Think...and think...while you are alive.

What you call 'salvation' belongs to the time before
death.

If you don't break your ropes while you're alive,

do you think ghosts will do it after?

The idea that the soul will join with the ecstatic

Just because the body is rotten -

that is all fantasy.

What is found now is found then.

If you find nothing now,

you will simply end up with an apartment in the City
of Death.

If you make love with the divine now, in the next life
you will have the face of satisfied desire.

So plunge into the truth, find out who the Teacher is

Believe in the Great Sound!

Kabir says this: When the guest is being searched for,

it is the intensity of the longing for the Guest that does all the work.

 Look at me, and you will see a slave of that intensity.

Kabir (trans. Robert Bly.)

We do not find God if we stay in the world. We do not find him if we leave the world. Whoever goes out with his whole being to meet his You, and carries to it all being that is in the world, finds Him who cannot be sought.

God is the wholly other; but He is also the wholly Same, the wholly Present…nearer to me than my I.

 Martin Buber

A chicken

To control the mosquito population, and so reduce the threat of malaria, has always been a major concern of the World Health Organization. A WHO group, working in Africa, hit on a scheme to educate the population to eliminate standing water, such as in pools, ponds and ditches. They created a movie of Africans using cans to carefully scoop out water, covering patches of water with earth, and draining ditches. They hoped that by showing the film to villagers in various parts of Africa, they would encourage them to follow suit, and so eliminate a fertile breeding ground for mosquitos.

They duly made the film, and arranged for its distribution as widely as possible.

After the film had been shown to a large number of Africans, one of the WHO workers suggested that they should get feedback from some of the people who had seen the film, and so determine the effectiveness of the project.

One of the WHO group sat down with an old African man and asked, "Now, what did you see?" "A chicken," said the old man. "A chicken?!" "Yes, a chicken!"

The WHO worker, rather bewildered, went back to the group and reported his finding. The rest of the group, equally bewildered, wondered what the old man was talking about. One of them said, "Why don't we review the film, and we might get some idea of what he had in mind?"

So they carefully replayed the film and, sure enough, part of the way through, for just a few frames, a chicken scampered across the bottom comer of the screen.

To see is to be

A full cup

Japanese Zen Master, Nan-in, one day was entertaining a university professor, who had come for instruction in Zen. As was the custom, Nan-in served tea. He poured tea into the visitor's cup and, when it was full, kept pouring. The professor watched this for a moment or two, and then exclaimed, "But, can't you see? The cup is full. You can't get any more in!" "This is just like your mind: you are so full of your own theories and opinions, how can you receive any instruction on Zen?"

No-one
Walks along this path
this autumn evening.
Baso

Governor Chu's visit

Governor Chu went one day to visit Zen Master Nansen. Arriving at the temple door, he presented his card to Nansen's assistant, and asked whether he could see the master. The assistant took the card, and the Governor awaited his return. After a short while, the assistant returned, and said, "I regret the master does not know you." "Nonsense! "Said Chu, "I come to visit him quite frequently. Please try again." The assistant left for a short while, and returning said again, "I regret that my master says that he does not know you." He returned the Governor's card to him.

The governor stood, quite perplexed for a while, turning the card over in his hand. All of a sudden he had an idea. Taking up a pen he crossed out the words 'Governor of the Province' and just left his name written on the card. "Would you please try one more time?" he asked the assistant.

The assistant once more took the card to Nansen. "This time he returned and said, "My master will be pleased to see you."

Who is the man of no rank?

A bowl of water

A monk, who was on pilgrimage, one night found he had nowhere to stay and, as it grew dark, he became concerned. While he was wondering where to sleep, he happened upon some caves in which a hermit had set up home. The hermit hospitably invited the monk to stay the night with him, an invitation that the monk gladly accepted. The hermit gave the monk some food and a bowl of water, which the monk drank with great relief.

In the morning, after the sun was up, the monk prepared to take leave of the hermit. The hermit, though, insisted that the monk be fed before leaving, and again gave him some food and a bowl of water. As he was drinking the water the monk noticed that the bowl was half a human skull and threw it to the ground in disgust.

"What sort of good for nothing monk are you?" demanded the hermit, "choosing this over that, that over this!" and threw the monk out.

We are the fools of time and terror: Days
Steal on us, and steal from us; yet we live,
Loathing our life, and yet dreading still to die.

The Prodigal Son

The Lotus Sutra tells of a young man who left his father's home and wandered off in search of experience. His father was a wealthy man, owning vast areas of land, abundant cattle, sheep, horses, and pigs. He had many servants and laborers working for him. His home was sumptuous, and contained riches of all kinds. After the son left home, the father searched for him in vain.

Meanwhile, the son wandered from country to country, his fortunes declining with the years. Through village after village he traveled, emaciated and worn, wearing ragged clothes, without any sense of direction, and without any goal in mind; now sleeping with the swine and eating the offal they at

The father continued to think of his son throughout the years of his absence, even though his son had been parted from him for more than 30 years. He declined to talk to others about his loss, and e. increasingly he began to think to himself, "I am now an old man worn with care. I own much wealth—gold, silver, and jewels, with granaries bursting, and treasuries overflowing

But I have lost my son. Some day I shall die, and my wealth will be scattered, lost with no-one to inherit it. Whenever he thought of his son, he would repeat over and over again to himself in sorrow, "If only I could find my son again, and commit my wealth to him, how happy I would be, how free of care and anxiety!

Meanwhile, the son worked wherever he could, and earned whatever pittance he was allowed. In his wandering, he unwittingly came again to his father's estate. Standing by the gate he saw his father from afar seated on a lion couch, his footstool a many jeweled cushion, revered and surrounded by learned men and worthy citizens. He wore jewels in a necklace around his neck, with rings on his fingers, and a brooch on his breast worth millions. Attendants and slaves with white fly whisks attended to his every need. A precious canopy covered him, from which hung streamers of flowers; perfume was sprinkled on the earth, and many more kinds of flowers were scattered around. Precious gifts were placed in rows, some of which he accepts and others he rejects. Such was his glory and honor.

The poor son, seeing this man possessed of such power, grew afraid, and regretted that he had made the mistake of coming to such a place. He said to himself, "This must be a king, or a person of high rank, I will never find employment here. I would be better off going to a poor hamlet where people would be more of my class. If I stay here I may be captured and enslaved."

Thinking in this way, he went to make good his escape. However, even though only seeing him from afar, his father had recognized his son immediately, and with great joy in his heart thought to himself, "Now at last, the one to whom I can bequeath my treasures has returned. For so long have I been thinking and dreaming of him with no way of making contact, and now, by himself, he has come, and my longing is at last satisfied."

He knew that his own lordly position in contrast to his son's poverty would cause his son distress. He tactfully says nothing about the young man being his son, but instead, wanting to entice him to stay, decides upon a strategy. Secretly, he sends two men of doubtful and undignified appearance saying, "Please go to such and such a place and say to the young man that you have work for him on this estate. If the young man agrees, and asks about the work he would be given, tell him he will be employed to remove a heap of dung, and that you will be

The two men went, found the son, and put the proposal to him. The son agreed, and, having received his wages beforehand, joined with them in working to remove the dung. The father, seeing from the distance his son's doleful and dirty figureworking alongside him." , gaunt and lean, is stricken with compassion for him. Taking off his jewels and fine clothes, and putting on instead coarse, torn and dirty garments, he smears his

body with dust, takes a shovel in his hands and goes to the laborers and says, "Get on with your work and don't be lazy!" Gradually, in this way he gets nearer to his son. When near enough, he calls to him saying, "Hey, you stay here and work. Do not go elsewhere, and I will increase your wages. You will also be given worn out clothes so that you can change those old tattered things you are wearing."

The son stays, and gradually his father promotes him into more responsible jobs, until he becomes the steward of the whole property. The old man, now near death, one day calls his son into his chambers and declares. "For a long time you have worked here on this land. Now at last I can claim you for what you are." He then embraced is son saying, "You are my son! You have traveled far, but your journeys are now done. You are home; you need suffer no more.

Lotus sutra

Long seeking it through others,
I was far from reaching it.
Now I go by myself;
I meet him everywhere.
He is just I myself,
But I am not he.

Understanding in this way,
I can be as I am

Tosan

The Prodigal Son²

Jesus continued: "There was a man who had two sons. The younger one said to his father, 'Father, give me my share of the estate.' So the father divided his property between his sons.

"Not long after, the younger son gathered together all he possessed, set off for a distant country, and there squandered his wealth in wild living. After he had lost all he had, a severe famine struck the whole country, and he fell into dire straits. In desperation he hired himself out to a citizen of that country, who sent him to the fields to feed pigs. The young son longed to fill his stomach with the pods that the pigs were eating, but no one gave him anything.

"When he came to his senses, he said, 'How many of my father's hired servants have food to spare, and here I am starving to death! I will set out and return to my father, and say to him: 'Father, I have sinned against heaven and against you. I am no longer worthy to be called your son; make me like one of your hired servants.' So he got up and went to his father.

"But while he was still a long way off, his father saw him and was filled with compassion for him; he ran to his son, threw his arms around him and kissed him.

"The son said to him, 'Father, I have sinned against heaven and against you. I am no longer worthy to be called your son.'

"But the father said to his servants, 'Quick! Bring the best robe and dress him in it. Put a ring on his finger, and sandals on his feet. Bring the fattened calf and kill it. Let's have a feast and celebrate. For this son of mine was dead and is alive again; he was lost and is found.' So they began to celebrate.

Meanwhile, the older son was in the field. When he came near the house, he heard music and dancing. So he called one of the servants and asked him what was happening. "Your brother has come back," he replied, "and your father has killed the fattened calf, because he has his son back, safe and sound."

The older brother became angry and refused to go in. So his father went out and pleaded with him. But he answered his father, "Look! All these years I've been slaving for you and never disobeyed your orders. Yet you never gave me even a young goat so I could celebrate with my friends. But when this son of yours, who has squandered your property on prostitutes, comes home, you kill the fattened calf for him!"

"My son," the father said, "you are always with me, and everything I have is yours. But we have to celebrate and be glad, because this brother of yours was dead and is alive again; he was lost and is found."

I was God inside God

Before I became Me.

I shall be God again

Once from that Me set free.

Angelus Silesius

Mullah prescribes
a prayer

A politician was gravely ill. He had heard about Mullah, who was supposed to have mystical abilities, and in his desperation decided to call Mullah in for help.

When Mullah arrived, the sick man said, "I have heard that you have mystical powers, and that you are in communication with higher beings. Please, Mullah, prescribe a prayer to help me when I pass over to the other side."

"With great pleasure!" exclaimed Mullah. "Here is your prayer: 'God help me; Devil help me.'"

Forgetting his illness, the patient sat upright in bed, and cried out, "Mullah, what are you saying? Are you mad?"

"Not a bit," said Mullah calmly. "Someone in your position cannot afford to take chances."

And if I laugh it is that I may not cry.

Children at play

It is like children playing by the sea. All day long they build sand castles with intricate moats and tall battlements. Each one claims a castle as his own. They fight to protect their castles, and to pull down the castles of others. They triumph and weep, triumph some more, and weep some more. Evening comes; the sun sinks low in the sky. The tide comes in. The children pick up their buckets and spades, turn around and go home.

The castles sink forgotten beneath the cold waves.

Life, like a dome of many colored glass,
Stains the white radiance of eternity.
Shelley.

Angelus Silesius

How brief our span!
Realizing this,
Why cause any man or beast
The least pain, the smallest grief.

A ruby, no lovelier
Than a rock;
An angel no more glorious
Than a frog.

> The moment you pause
> To rest on the Way,
> You slip behind;
> Pulled back,
> You go astray

See what no eye sees
Go where no foot goes
Choose what is no choice
Now, you may hear no sound:
God's voice

"The universe and you are of the same root: you and every single thing are a unity. The gurgle of the stream, the sigh of the wind: the voices of the master. The green of pine, the white of snow: the colors of the master...the very one who lifts the hands, moves the legs, sees, hears. The One who grasps this directly without the need of reason or thought has some inner realization." Bassui.

Do not mistake the finger for the moon.

Q.　　As for the finger I will not ask you about it. But what is the moon?

A. Where is the finger that you will not ask me about?

Q. As for the moon I will not ask you about it. But what is the finger?

A. The moon.

The monk challenged and said, "I asked about the finger why should you answer me 'the moon?"

A. Because you asked me about the finger!

A tangle within, a tangle without
This world is entangled in a tangle.

Benoit on Humility[3]

The whole problem of human suffering is summed up by the problem of humiliation. Freedom from suffering is freedom from the possibility of being humiliated. From where does humiliation come? From seeing myself powerless? No, that is not enough. It comes because I try in vain not to see my real powerlessness.

Powerlessness itself does not cause humiliation; it is caused by the shock I experience when my claim to be unique comes up against the reality of things. I am not humiliated because the world denies me, but because I am unable to overcome this denial. The cause of my suffering never lies in the outside world; it is the result of the claim that I make, and which is broken against the wall of reality. I deceive myself when I say that the world has thrown itself against me and hurt me; it is I who have hurt myself. When I no longer claim uniqueness, nothing will ever hurt me again.

If a humiliating experience turns up, offering me a marvelous opportunity to see into myself, at once the imagination throws up some supposed danger. In short I constantly defend myself against that which offers to save me; I fight inch by inch to protect the very source of my unhappiness.

I will stop fighting against the constructive and harmonizing benefits of humiliation to the degree to which I can understand that my true well being is to be found, paradoxically, where, until now, I have thought my pain resided.

If I understand, I will resist less and less. In this way, I will see more often that I am humiliated, because I will see that all my negative states are, at bottom, humiliations. I will then be able to feel myself humiliated, annoyed, without any image arising in me, other than this state, and will be able to remain there motionless, my understanding having rid me of the reflex attempts at flight. From the moment that I succeed in no longer moving in my humiliated state, I discover to my surprise that *there* is an 'asylum of rest,' the unique harbor of safety, the only place in the world in which I can find complete security. I feel myself nearer to the ground, nearer to real humility, humility that is not the acceptance of my inferiority, but the abandonment of my claim to be unique. These inner phenomena are accompanied by a feeling of sadness, of 'night' and this feeling is quite different from the sadness of suffering because a great calm reigns therein.

Free at last! a monk on the road,
 Where is the old Zen barrier?
 My life: water-and-cloud leaving no trace,
 Which mountain shall be my home?
   Manan (1591-1654)

Bodhidharma on suffering

If a follower of the **way** falls into any kind of suffering or trial one should think and say thus:

"During countless past ages I have abandoned the root and gone after the branches, carried along on the restless, bitter waves of the sea of existence, and have, because of this, created endless occasions for hate, ill-will and wrong-doing. The harm done has been limitless. Although my present suffering may not be caused by any wrongdoing committed in this life, yet it is the fruit of my errors in a past existence that happens to ripen at this moment. *It is not something that men or gods have given to me.* Let me therefore take, patiently and sweetly, this bitter fruit of my own making without resentment or complaint against anyone or anything."

When this way of thinking is awakened the mind responds spontaneously to the dictates of Reason, so that this can even help one make use of other people's hatred and so turn it into an occasion to advance toward the Tao. This is called "the rule of the repayment of debts."

> Bodhidharma

Sentimentality is enjoying an emotion for which one has not paid the price. Oscar Wilde

Martin Buber

The free person is the one who wills without arbitrary self will. He believes in destiny and believes that it stands in need of him…he must go to it, yet does not know where it is to be found. But he does know that he must go out with his whole being. He does not interfere, but at the same time he does not let things merely happen. He listens to what is emerging from himself, to the course of being in the world; not in order to be supported by it, but in order to bring it to reality as it desires.

Martin Buber

When the wooden man sings his song,
The stone maiden moves to dance.

Intentional suffering and conscious labour

Rinzai

It is not that I understood from the moment I was born, but that, after exhaustive investigation and grinding discipline, in an instant I knew myself.

Bodhidharma

The incomparable truth of the Buddhas can only be attained by immeasurable striving, practicing what cannot be practiced, and bearing the unbearable.

Hakuin

If you keep on doubting continuously, with a bold spirit and a sense of shame urging you on, your effort will naturally become unified and solid, turning into a single mass of doubt throughout heaven and earth. The spirit will feel suffocated, the mind distressed, like a bird in a cage, like a rat that has gone into a bamboo tube and cannot escape.

F. H. Bradley

The shades nowhere speak without blood and the ghosts of Metaphysic accept no substitute. They reveal themselves only to that victim whose life they have drained, and, to converse with shadows he himself must become a shadow.

The person whose nature is such that by one path alone his desire will reach consummation, will try to find it on that path whatever it might be, and whatever the world thinks of it; and, if he does not, he is contemptible. Self-sacrifice is too often the great' sacrifice of trade, the giving cheap what is worth nothing. To know what one wants, and to scruple at no means that will get it, may be a harder self-surrender.

Commitment

Until one is committed there is hesitancy,

the chance to draw back, always ineffectiveness.

Concerning all acts of initiative (and creation),

there is one elementary truth, the ignorance of which

kills countless ideas and splendid plans:

that the moment one definitely commits oneself,

then Providence moves too.

All sorts of things occur to help one

that would never otherwise have occurred.

A whole stream of events issues from the decision,

raising in one's favor all manner of unforeseen incidents

and meetings and material assistance,

which no person could have dreamt would have come

their way.

W.H.Murray

Everyday Mind

Word spread across the countryside about the wise Holy Man who lived in a small house atop the mountain. A man from the village decided to make the long and difficult journey to visit him. When he arrived at the house, he saw an old servant inside, who greeted him at the door.

"I would like to see the wise Holy Man," he said to the servant. The servant smiled and led him inside. As they walked through the house, the man from the village looked eagerly around the house, anticipating his encounter with the Holy Man. Before he knew it, he had been led to the back door, and escorted outside. He stopped, and turned to the servant, "But I want to see the Holy Man!" "You already have," said the old man. "Everyone you may meet in life, even if they appear plain and insignificant...see each of them as a wise Holy Man. If you do this, then whatever problem you brought here today will be solved."

Joshu: What is the Way?
Zen Master Nansen: Every day mind is the Way
Mumonkan.

Nisargadatta

Whatever name you give it: will, or steady purpose, or one pointedness of mind, you come back to earnestness, sincerity, honesty. When you are in dead earnest, you bend every incident, every second of your life to your purpose. You do not waste time and energy on other things; you are totally dedicated, call it will or love or plain honesty. We are complex beings at war within and without. We contradict ourselves all the time undoing today the work of yesterday. No wonder we are stuck. A little integrity would make a lot of difference.

Become present as yourself; become aware of your own existence. See how you function, be present to the motives and the results of your actions. Get to know the prison you have built around yourself by inadvertence. By knowing what you are not you come to know your self.

The way back to your self is through refusal and rejection. One thing is certain; the real is not imaginary, it is not a product of the mind. Even the sense "I am" is not continuous, though it is a useful pointer; it shows where to seek, but not what to seek. Just get to know it completely.

The sweet melon is sweet, through and through; the bitter melon is bitter through and through.

Nobody really knows

Suddenly realizing that he did not know who he was, Mullah Nasrudin rushed into the street, looking for someone who might recognize him.

The crowds were thick, but he was in a strange town, and he found no familiar face.

Suddenly he found himself in a carpenter's shop. 'What can I do for you?' asked the craftsman, stepping forward. Nasrudin said nothing.

'Perhaps you would like something made from wood?'

'First things first.' said the Mullah. 'Now, did you see me come into your shop?'

'Yes, I did.'

'Good. Now, have you ever seen me in your life before?'

'Never in my life.'

'Then how do you know it is me?'

Enquiring, 'Who am I that is in bondage?' and knowing one's real nature alone, is liberation.

> Ramana Maharshi

St. John of the Cross

When they get a glimpse of this concrete and perfect life of the spirit—which manifests itself in the complete absence of all sweetness, in aridity, distaste and in the many trials that are the true spiritual cross—they flee from it as from death. What they seek in their communion with God is sweet and delectable feelings; but this is a sort of spiritual gluttony rather than self-denial and spiritual poverty. As far as their spirituality is concerned, they become enemies of Christ. They seek themselves in God, which is the very opposite of love; for to seek oneself in God is to seek favors and refreshing delights of God, where as to seek God in oneself is to incline oneself to choose for Christ's sake, all that is most distasteful; and this is love of God.

"When the mountains close in on you on every side from all four directions...what then?"

"It is the pathless that is Joshu!"

> *Joshu*

Mullah's New Shirt

Mullah decided to buy himself a new shirt. He carefully saved his money until he had enough to buy it. At last, with some excitement and trepidation, he went off to the tailor's to be measured for the shirt. After measuring him the tailor said, "Come back in a week's time and, God willing, the shirt will be ready."

Mullah went home, and for the week waited in anticipation for his shirt to be ready. He finally went back to the tailor's to collect it.

"There has been some delay. However, if God wills it, your shirt will be ready in a couple of days.

After two days Mullah returned to get his shirt.

"I am so sorry, the shirt is not yet ready, come back tomorrow and, if God wills it, it will be ready."

"How long would it take," asked Mullah in desperation, "if you leave God out of it?"

A monk asked, "How can you tell what is true before the blossoming of awakening?"

"It is blossoming now," replied the master.

Is That So?

Hakuin was admired by his neighbors for living a clean, upright life.

The daughter of one of the neighbors was found to be pregnant.

Her parents were very angry. However, the girl refused to say who was the father. Finally, after a great deal of harassment, she said that the father was Hakuin.

The parents went to the master in a great rage. "Is that so?" was all he said.

After the child was born, the parents brought it to Hakuin to look after. He had, by this time, lost his good reputation. He was quite untroubled by this, but looked after the baby carefully, getting food and milk from the neighbors as best he could.

Some many months later, the girl gave in and confessed the truth. The real father was a local young man who worked in the village.

The girl's parents immediately went to Hakuin to ask his forgiveness. They apologized at length, and asked for the baby to be returned.

Hakuin agreed. In giving up the child, all he said was: "Is that so?"

Magnificent! magnificent!
No-one knows the final word.
The ocean bed's aflame,
Out of the void leap wooden lambs. Satori poem

Teaching Reality

Mullah was teaching a class at school, and one of his students asked, "Who did the best thing: the one who conquered an empire, the one who could have done so but refrained from doing it, or a third who prevented someone else from doing so."

Mullah replied, "I do not know about these things. But I do have an even harder question to answer,"

"What is that," asked the student.

"How can I teach you to see things as they really are?"

She goes into the lake without making a ripple;
She walks in the woods without disturbing a blade of grass.

Tozan

A monk asked Tozan, "How can we avoid the cold in winter and the heat in summer?" Tozan asked, "Why do you not go where there is no heat in summer or cold in winter?" "Where is such a place?" asked the monk. Tozan said, "When it is cold shiver, when it is hot, sweat."

The only hope, or else despair
Lies in the choice of pyre of pyre-
To be redeemed from fire by fire.
T.S.Eliot

Cloud of Unknowing

Strike that thick cloud of unknowing with the sharp dart of longing love, and on no account whatever think of giving up. When you first begin, you find only darkness, and, as it were, a cloud of unknowing. Reconcile yourself to wait in this darkness as long as is necessary, but still go on longing after that which you love." "So there is strife and pain on every side. Work hard at it, therefore and with all speed; hammer away at this high cloud of unknowing—and take your rest later! It is hard work and no mistake, very hard work indeed. Oh everybody finds this work hard.

Cry to him with a yearning heart, and then you will see him. After the rosy light of dawn out comes the sun; likewise, longing is followed by the vision of God. He will reveal himself to you if you love him with the combined force of the three attachments: the attachment if the miser to his money, the attachments of a mother to her newborn babe, and the attachment of the lover to the beloved.

   Ramakrishna

Sei and her Soul

In a place called Koyo lived a man, Chokan, whose daughter, Sei, was very beautiful, and the pride of her father. She had a handsome cousin named Ochu. Chokan, as a joke, used to say they would make a fine married couple. The two young people, being in love with each other, took this chaffing seriously, and thought of themselves as engaged. The father, however, intended to give her in marriage to another young man, Hinryo, and tragedy could not be avoided.

When Ochu heard of Chokan's intention, he left the place by boat, indignant and angry. After several days journey he found to his astonishment that Sei was on the same boat. Overjoyed they went to the country of Shoku, where they lived for several years, and there had two children. Sei, however, could not forget her native land. She felt that she had deserted her father, and wondered what he thought of her. She wanted to return home, so her husband decided to go back together with her.

When they arrived back at the home island, Ochu asked Sei to wait in the boat while he went to make peace with her father. Arriving at the house, Ochu apologized to the father for taking his daughter away from her home, and begged him to forgive them. "What is the meaning of all this?" exclaimed the father. "What woman are you talking about?" "Sei," replied Ochu. "Nonsense!" said Chokan. " After you left, Sei became ill and has been in bed for several years. You cannot be talking about Sei!! Sei has not spoken and has lain in bed as if in a stupor."

Ochu went back to the boat to find Sei, and took her to the father's house.

When Sei came from the boat, Sei — lying in bed — being told of this, arose from her bed, went towards her and the two became one.

Sei and her soul are separated, which is the true Sei?

I am the first and the last.

I am the honored one and the scorned one.

I am the harlot and the holy one.

I am the wife and the virgin.

I am the mother and the daughter

I am she whose wedding is great and

I have not taken a husband

Gnostic verse

Nansen and the Governor

After they had finished a retreat, Zen master Nansen and the Governor of the province were walking in the monastery garden.

Nansen turned to the governor, and asked, "How will you now govern the province?"

"With wisdom and compassion," declared the Governor.

"Then every last one will suffer," retorted Nansen.

O my God, how does it happen in this poor world that Thou art so great and yet nobody finds thee, Thou art so near yet nobody feels Thee, that Thou give thyself to everyone and nobody knows Thy name? Men flee from Thee and say they cannot find Thee; they turn their back and say they cannot see Thee; they stop their ears and say they cannot hear Thee.

Buddha Said

There is that sphere wherein is neither earth nor water, fire nor air: It is not the infinity of space, nor the infinity of perception; it is not nothingness, nor is it neither idea nor non-idea; it is neither this world nor the next, nor is it both; it is neither the sun nor the moon.

It neither comes nor goes, it is neither permanent nor impermanent; it is not caused, established, begun, supported; it is the end of suffering.

Whatever you do is of no use.

Now, What will you do?

Zen Master

Ramana Maharshi

Every living being longs always to be happy, untainted by sorrow; and every one has the greatest love for him or herself, which is solely due to the fact that happiness is one's real nature. Hence in order to realize that inherent and untainted happiness, which indeed one daily experiences when the mind is subdued in deep sleep, it is essential that one should know oneself. For obtaining such knowledge the enquiry, "Who am I?" in quest of the Self is the best means.

In Spring, the flowers,
the cool breezes in summer ,
In autumn the moon.
The snow in winter.
    Mumon

Egotism

The Prime Minister of the Tang Dynasty was a national hero for his success as both a statesman and military leader. But despite his fame, power, and wealth, he considered himself a humble and devout Buddhist. Often he visited his favorite Zen master to study under him, and they seemed to get along very well. The fact that he was prime minister apparently had no effect on their relationship, which seemed to be simply one of a revered master and respectful student. One day, during his usual visit, the Prime Minister asked the master, "Your Reverence, what is egotism according to Buddhism?" The master's face turned red, and in a very condescending and insulting tone of voice, he shot back, "What kind of stupid question is that!?" This unexpected response so shocked the Prime Minister that he became sullen and angry. The Zen master then smiled, and said, "That, Your Excellency, is egotism."

Whirled by the three passions, one's eyes go blind;
Closed to the world of things, they see again.
In this way I live; straw-hatted, staff in hand,
I move illimitably, through earth, through heaven.
Ungo (1580-1659)

The chief difficulty

The chief difficulty in the way of liberation from whole entire slavery consists in this: it is necessary, with an intention issuing from one's own initiative and persistence, and sustained by one's own efforts, that is to say, not by another's will but one's own, to obtain the eradication from one's presence both of the already fixed consequences of certain properties of that something which is called the ego as well as the predisposition to those consequences which may again arise.

The consequences of maintaining 'I am unique' are: arrogance, the need to provoke astonishment in others, bragging, cunning, the vice of eating, egoism, envy, hate, imagination, jealousy, lying, offensiveness, partiality, pride, wishing the death or weakness of others, self-conceit, self love, swagger, vanity, slyness, ambition, double-facedness.

     Gurdjieff

Gurdjieff's solution

The sole means now for saving the beings of the planet Earth would be to implant again into their presence a new organ of such properties that everyone of these unfortunates during the process of existence should constantly sense and be cognizant of the inevitability of his own death as well as of the death of everyone upon whom his eyes or attention rests

In praise of Krshna

O! Madhava, how shall I tell you of my terror?
I could not describe my coming here
If I had a million tongues.
When I left my room and saw the darkness
I trembled:
I could not see the path,
there were snakes that writhed round my ankles!

I was alone, a woman; the night was so dark, the forest
so dense and gloomy, and I had so far to go.
The rain was pouring down— which path should I
take? My feet were muddy
and burning where thorns had scratched them.
But I had the hope of seeing you, none of it mattered,
and now my terror seems far away .
When the sound of your flute reaches my ears it com-
pels me to leave my home, my friends, it draws me into the dark toward you.

I no longer count the pain of coming here,

says Govinda-dasa.

*Pai Chang said at his monastery were three
secrets: drink tea, take care and rest.*

Samadhi

Rapt in Beethoven's music, I closed my eyes and watched a silver glow, which shaped itself into a circle with a central focus brighter than the rest. The circle became a tunnel of light proceeding from some distant sun in the heart of the Self. Swiftly and smoothly I was borne through the tunnel, and as I went the light turned from silver to gold. There was an impression of drawing strength from a limitless sea of power, and a sense of deepening peace. The light grew brighter, but was never dazzling or alarming. I came to a point where time and motion ceased. In my recollection it took the shape of a flat-topped rock, surrounded by a summer sea, with a sandy pool at its foot. The dream scene vanished and I am absorbed in the Light of the Universe, in Reality glowing like fire with the knowledge of itself, without ceasing to be one and myself, merged like a drop of quicksilver in the Whole, yet still separate as a grain of sand in the desert. The peace that passes all understanding and the pulsating energy of creation are one in the center in the midst of conditions where all opposites are reconciled.

From Warner Allen, The Timeless Moment (Faber and Faber)

Monk: How can we avoid life and death?

Master: Where are you?

Samadhi 2

I had spent the evening in a great city (London 1872) with two friends, reading and discussing poetry and philosophy. We parted at midnight. I had a long drive in a hansom to my lodging. My mind, deeply under the influence of the ideas, images and emotions called up by the reading and talk, was calm and peaceful. I was in a state of quiet, almost passive enjoyment, not actually thinking, but letting images and emotions flow of themselves as it were though my mind.

All at once, without warning of any kind, I found myself wrapped in a flame-coloured cloud. For an instant I thought of fire, an immense conflagration somewhere close by in that great city; the next instant I knew that that fire was in myself. Directly afterwards, there came upon me a sense of exultation, of immense joyousness, accompanied or immediately followed by an intellectual illumination quite impossible to describe. Among other things, I did not merely come to believe, I saw that the universe is not composed of dead matter, but is, on the contrary, a living Presence; I became conscious in myself of eternal life. It was not a conviction that I would have eternal life, but a consciousness that I possessed eternal life then; I saw that all men are

immortal; that the cosmic order is such that without any peradventure all things work together for the good of each and all; that the foundation principle of the world, of all the worlds, is what we call love, and that the happiness of each and all is in the long run certain.

The vision lasted a few seconds and was gone; but the memory of it, and the sense of the reality of it have remained during the quarter of a century that has since elapsed. I knew that what the vision showed was true. I had attained to a point of view from which I saw that it must be true. That view, that conviction, I may say that consciousness has never, even during the periods of the deepest depression, been lost.

R.M.Bucke

By oneself evil is done,
By oneself one suffers
By oneself evil is undone
No-one can purify another.

Buddha

Destiny

During a momentous battle, a Japanese general decided to attack even though his army was greatly outnumbered. He was confident they would win, but his men were filled with doubt. On the way to the battle, they stopped at a religious shrine. After praying with the men, the general took out a coin and said, "I shall now toss this coin. If it is heads, we shall win. If tails, we shall lose. Destiny will now reveal itself." He threw the coin into the air and all watched intently as it landed. It was heads. The soldiers were so overjoyed and filled with confidence that they vigorously attacked the enemy and were victorious. After the battle, a lieutenant remarked to the general, "No one can change destiny." "Quite right," the general replied as he showed the lieutenant the coin, which had heads on both sides.

If 'tis now, 'tis not to be,
if 'tis to be, 'tis not now
The ripeness is all!

Dietrich Bonheoffer

(Dietrich Bonheoffer was a German pastor who was imprisoned and executed for opposing Nazism. He wrote the following in prison.)

Who am I? They often tell me
I step from my cell's confinement
calmly, cheerfully, firmly,
like a squire from his country-house.
Who am I? They often tell me
I talk to my warders
freely and friendly and clearly,
as though it were mine to command.
Who am I? They also tell me
I bear the days of misfortune
equably, smilingly, proudly
like one accustomed to win.

Am I then really all that which other men tell of?
Or am I only what I know of myself,
restless and longing and sick, like a bird in a cage,
struggling for breath, as though hands were compressing my throat,
yearning for colors, for flowers, for the voices of birds,
thirsting for words of kindness, for neighborliness,
tossing in expectation of great events,
powerlessly trembling for friends at an infinite distance,
weary and empty at praying, at thinking, at making,
faint, and ready to say farewell to it all?
Who am I? This or the other?
Am I one person today, and tomorrow another?

Am I both at once? A hypocrite before others,
and before myself a contemptibly woebegone weakling?
Or is something within me still like a beaten army,
fleeing in disorder from victory already achieved?

Who am I? They mock me, these lonely questions of mine.
Whoever I am, you know, O God, I am yours.

The falling leaves
fall and pile up; the rain
beats on the rain.

Exertion

Bodhidharma

The incomparable "Marvelous Tao of all the Buddhas," is attained only by long diligence in a practice difficult to practice, and by long endurance of that which it is difficult to endure.

Shibayama

You who have not spent sleepless nights in suffering and tears, who do not know the experience of being unable to swallow even a piece of bread—the grace of God will never reach you.

Buddha

My Doctrine implies thinking of that which is beyond thought, performing that which is beyond performance, speaking of that which is beyond words, and practicing that which is beyond practice.

Dogen

The great way of the Buddha and the Patriarchs involves the highest form of exertion which goes on unceasingly in cycles from the first dawning of religious truth, through the test of discipline and practice to awakening and Nirvana. It is sustained exertion proceeding without lapse from cycle to cycle. Accordingly it is exertion that is neither self imposed, nor imposed by others, but free and uncoerced. The merit of this exertion upholds me and upholds others.

The truth is that the benefits of one's own struggles and sustained exertions are shared by all beings in the ten directions. Others may not be aware of this, and we may not realize it ourselves, but it is so. It is through the sustained exertions of the Buddhas and Patriarchs that our own exertions are made possible, that we are able to reach the high road of Truth. In exactly the same way, it is through our own exertions that the exertions of the Buddhas are made possible, and that the Buddhas attain the high road of Truth

This exertion too sustains the sun, moon and the stars; it sustains the earth and sky, body and mind, object and subject, the four elements and five skandhas

The merits of these exertions are sometimes disclosed and thus arises the dawn of religious consciousness, which is then tested in practice. Sometimes, however, these merits lie hidden and are neither seen nor heard nor realized. Yet hidden though they may be, they are still available, because they suffer no diminution or restriction, whether they are visible or invisible, tangible or intangible.

At this moment a flower blossoms, a leaf falls — it is a manifestation of sustained exertion. A mirror is brightened, a mirror is broken — it is a manifestation of sustained exertion. Everything is exertion. To attempt to avoid exertion is an impossible evasion because the attempt itself is exertion. This sustained exertion is not something that people of the world naturally love or desire, yet it is the last refuge of all.

> *"Followers of the way, in the Buddha dharma, no effort is necessary. Just be your ordinary selves: relieving yourselves, putting on clothes, eating food, lying down to sleep when tired."*
>
> *Rinzai*

A Samurai Visited Hakuin.

A samurai visited Hakuin and asked: "Does heaven and hell really exist?"

"Who are you?" asked Hakuin.

"I am a samurai," the man replied.

"You, a warrior!" shouted Hakuin. "What kind of lord would employ you? You have a crafty look about you."

The samurai became so enraged that he started to draw his sword. Hakuin jeered: "So you own a sword! It is probably much too blunt to hurt me."

The samurai drew out his sword. Hakuin said: "Here open the gates of hell!"

Hearing this the samurai, recognizing the master's discipline, put his sword away and bowed.

"Here open the gates of paradise," said Hakui

If your eye is single your whole body is filled with light.

Jesus

Layman P'ang

Master Shih-Tou said to the Layman: "Since we last met, what have you been doing during the day?

"When you ask me about what I have been doing, I can't open my mouth," the Layman replied.

"That is why I am asking you," said Shih T'ou.

Whereupon the Layman offered this verse:

What I do during the day is not unusual,
I'm just naturally in harmony with them.
Grasping nothing, discarding nothing,
In every place there's no obstruction, no conflict.
What is there that is exalted in that?
From the hills and mountains, the last speck of dust is cleared away
My miraculous power and magical activity,
Drawing water and carrying firewood.

The poppy flowers
How calmly
They fall.

The Arrow of the Heart

After winning several archery contests, the young and rather boastful champion challenged a Zen master, who was renowned for his skill as an archer. The young man demonstrated remarkable technical proficiency when he hit a distant bull's eye on his first try, and then split that arrow with his second shot. "There," he said to the old man, "see if you can match that!"

Undisturbed, the master did not draw his bow, but rather motioned for the young archer to follow him up the mountain. Curious about the old fellow's intentions, the champion followed him high into the mountain until they reached a deep chasm, spanned by a rather Calmly stepping out onto the middle of the unsteady and certainly perilous bridge, the old master picked a far away tree as a target, drew his bow, and fired a clean, direct hit. "Now it is your turn," he said as he gracefully stepped back onto the safe ground.flimsy and shaky log.

Staring with terror into the seemingly bottomless and beckoning abyss, the young man could not force himself to step out onto the log, no less shoot at a target. "You have much skill with your bow," the master said, sensing his challenger's predicament, "but you have little skill with the mind that lets loose the shot."

> *Your love of others is the result of self-knowledge, not its cause.*
>
> *Nisargadatta.*

Jesus said,

If those who lead you say to you
Lo, the kingdom is in heaven,
then the birds of heaven will precede you,
If they say to you,
It is in the sea,
then the fish will precede you,
But the kingdom is within you and outside you,
When you know yourselves then you will be known
and you will know that you are the sons of the living Father.
But if you do not know yourselves
then you are in poverty, and you are poverty.

Q. What is the realm in which there is neither day nor night?
Joshu. Is it day now? Is it night now?
Q. I am not asking about now!
Joshu. You cannot do away with me.

Learning Fast

Once upon time a donkey, fox, and lion agreed they would help one another to hunt for food. Together they would be sure that all would survive. The fox and donkey were somewhat nervous about going on a hunt with the lion, but, thinking about the food they would get with the lion's help, they overcame their fears The hunt was very successful.

They came to a clearing by a lake and, after they had agreed upon a plan, they separated. The plan was that they would search through the jungle looking for prey. The donkey would keep a watch for animals to attack; after he found one, he was to introduce himself. The introductory bray would alert the other two, who were hiding. The fox would come out at first, growling at the animal. The frightened animal would try to run, the fox would give chase, and in trying to avoid him, the animal would run directly into the path of the lion. The lion would then finish the animal off in one swoop.

In the evening, the three of them assembled in front of the lion's den with their bounteous harvest. The lion told the donkey to give to each of the three hunters his fair share, according to their agreement. The donkey was very pleased about this, as he believed that by honoring him in this way, the lion had shown confidence in him. Very carefully, he shared the catch into three equal amounts.

"Sirs, I have done what was necessary. Would you now kindly take your share." The lion considered his share for just a moment and said, "Do you really believe that each deserves an equal share! Do you think that your ridiculous job of chatting with the prey is equal to my contribution, which was to kill them?" Saying this he leapt on the donkey and killed him in a moment.

He then ordered the terrified fox to share the spoils. The fox gathered the entire kill in one large pile, and kept the least amount for himself. He asked the lion to take the large pile. "Who has instructed you in the art of division? You have got it right down to the smallest fraction," beamed the happy lion. "The donkey made an admirable instructor, Sir," said the fox.

There is a fine saying of one heathen philosopher to another about this, he says: "I am aware of something in me which sparkles in my intelligence; I clearly perceive that it is somewhat but what I cannot grasp. Yet methinks if only I could seize it I should know all truth."

Meister Eckhart.

Ma Tsu

The Patriarch said to the assembly, "All of you should know that your mind is Buddha, that this mind is identical with Buddha. "Those who seek the Dharma should not seek for anything. Outside of mind there is no other Buddha, outside of Buddha there is no other mind. Not attaching to good and not rejecting evil, without reliance on either purity or defilement, one realizes that the nature of karma is empty. It cannot be found in each thought because it is without self-nature. Therefore, the three realms are mind-only and all phenomena in the universe are marked by a single Dharma. " Whenever we see form, it is just seeing the mind. The mind does not exist by itself; its existence is due to form. Whatever you are seeing, it is just a phenomenon, which is identical with the principle. All forms are without obstruction, and the fruit of the way to Bodhi is also like that.

"Whatever arises in the mind is called form. When one knows all forms to be empty then birth is one with no-birth. If one realizes this mind, then one can always wear one's robes and eat one's food. Nourishing the womb of wisdom, one spontaneously passes one's time: what else is there to do? Having received my teaching, listen to my verse:

"Bodhi is just peace.

When phenomena and the principle are all without obstruction,

The very birth is identical with no-birth."

If any seek me in form
If any seek me in sound
He walks the wrong path
He can never see the Buddha
Diamond Sutra

How the mighty have fallen

A huge tree grew at the edge of a forest. It spread out its great branches and powerful roots. Its bounteous leaves provided shelter from the sun to many creatures; it provided a home for numerous birds and countless small animals. It buzzed with life all the time. A little plant grew at its base. It was a delicate willow that would bend at the touch of even the lightest breeze.

One day, the two trees were having a discussion. "You are so small and weak," said the great tree, "why do you not thrust your roots deeply into the ground, and lift your branches high into the sky? Look at me, at how powerful and strong I am."

"That is not my way," smiled the tree. "You see I am safer like this."

"Ho!" snorted the tree, "Do you think, puny as you are, that you are safer than me with all my power and strength! See how deeply I have buried my roots, and how powerful is my trunk. Nothing could ever make me bow my head to the ground as yours is bowed at every puff of wind." And the discussion abruptly ended.

But the small tree was to have the last word. One night a fierce hurricane struck the region. Hurtling trees to the ground after tearing up their roots, the hurricane raged destruction through the forest. The great tree was uprooted, and crashed to the ground.

After the storm had blown itself out, the villagers came to see the damage. Majestic trees whose branches had reached high into the heavens had been struck down, and lay crumbled and smashed onto the ground. They lay like the dead and wounded on the battlefields after the battle has passed: except for one plant. The small neighbor of the great tree had been battered and beaten by the hurricane, but each time it had bent under the fury of the onslaught. After the hurricane had relented and left, the little plant had sighed with relief. It then stood up straight again. Where there had been a mighty neighbor, there was now just the open sky.

Yield to the willow all the longing,
all the loathing of your heart

Nisargadatta

You are the Supreme reality beyond the world and its creator, beyond consciousness and its witness, beyond all assertions and denials. Remember it, think of it, act on it. Abandon all sense of separation, see yourself in all, and act accordingly. With action, bliss will come, and with bliss, conviction. After all, you doubt yourself because you are in sorrow. Happiness — natural, spontaneous and lasting — cannot be imagined. Either it is there or it is not. Once you begin to experience the peace, love and happiness, which need no outer cause, all your doubts will dissolve. Just catch hold of what I told you, and live by it.

The outer teacher gives the instructions, the inner sends the strength; the alert application is the student's. Without will, intelligence and energy on the part of the student the outer teacher is helpless. The inner teacher bides his chance. Obtuseness and wrong pursuits bring about a crisis, and the disciple awakens to his own plight. Wise is the one who does not wait for a shock, which can be quite rude. The inner teacher is not committed to non-violence. He can be quite violent at times to the point of destroying the obtuse or perverted personality. Suffering and death, as well as life and happiness, are his tools of work. It is only in duality that non-violence becomes the unifying law

This does not mean that one should be afraid of the inner teacher. It means well but must be taken seriously. It calls for attention and obedience; when it is not listened to it turns from persuasion to compulsion, for while it can wait it shall not be denied. The difficulty lies not with the teacher, inner or outer. The teacher is always available. It is the ripe student that is lacking. When a person is not ready what can be done?

It has no form and yet it appears

Zen Master Daito

All of you who have come to this mountain monastery, do not forget that you are here for the sake of the way, not for the sake of food and clothing...Apply yourselves throughout the day to knowing the unknowable. From start to finish, investigate all things in detail. Time flies like an arrow, so do not waste energy on trivial matters. Be attentive! Be attentive!

After this old monk completes his pilgrimage, some of you may preside over grand temples with magnificent buildings and huge libraries adorned with gold and silver and have many followers. Others may devote themselves to sutra study, esoteric chants, continual meditation, and strict observance of the precepts.

Whatever the course of action, if the mind is not set on the marvelous transcendent way of the Buddhas and Patriarchs, causality is negated, and the teaching collapses. Such people are devils and can never be my true heirs. The one who tends to his own affairs and clarifies his own nature, even though he may be residing in the remote countryside in a hut, subsisting on wild roots and vegetables cooked in an old battered cauldron, encounters my tradition, daily receives my teaching with gratitude. Who can take this lightly? Work harder! Work harder!

A glass of wine

Thieves broke into a Japanese Zen Temple, threatening to rob the place and kill the priest. Faced with their threats, the priest held up his hand declaring, "I must have one last glass of wine." Turning his back on the thieves, he went to a cupboard, opened the door, and carefully took down a bottle of wine and a small glass, both of which he placed neatly in the center of a low table. Returning to the cupboard he took out a cloth, closed the door, and, returning, knelt down at the table, where he quietly polished the glass with the cloth. He poured out a small measure of wine, carefully put the cork back in the bottle, and set the bottle again at the center of the table. He then proceeded to drink the wine, savoring fully each sip. Finishing the last drop of wine, he stood up, preparing to wash the glass. He looked around the room. The thieves had left.

Words are wise men's counters, they do but reckon by them: but they are the money of fools."

Hobbes

Gospel according to Thomas

If two make peace with one another in the
same house,
they will say to the mountain,
Move! and it will move.

I am the light, which is over everything.
I am the all;
(from me) the All has gone forth,
and to me the all had returned.
Split wood: I am there
Lift up the stone, and Iyou will find me there

He who is near me is near the fire,
and he who is far from me
is far from the kingdom

"The good Gautama neither knows nor sees suffering."

"It is not that I do not know suffering, do not see it. I know it I see it."

The entire universe
is your eye

The entire universe is your eye; the entire universe is your complete body; the entire universe is your own light; the entire universe is within your own light. In the entire universe there is no one who is not your own self. I repeat what I am continually saying to you: All the Buddhas of the Three Worlds and all the sentient beings in the Dharmadhatu, these are the light of the Great Intrinsic Wisdom.

Chosha

The eye with which I see God is the eye with which God sees me

Meister Eckhart

A disciple said to Buddha

I have such faith in the master that I believe there has never been, nor will there be, nor is there now any other, whether ascetic or Brahman, who is greater and wiser than the Master, that is to say as regards the higher wisdom.

You speak grandly and boldly, Sariputra. Indeed quite a paean of ecstasy! So you must have known all the Masters of the past who were arhats and Buddhas, and you must be able to comprehend their minds and know their actions, their wisdom, their way of life, and the great release that they attained?

No, sir.

And you must have perceived also all the Masters of the future who shall be arhats and Buddhas, and be able to comprehend their minds and actions, their wisdom, and way of life, and the great release they shall attain?

No, sir.

Well at least, then, Sariputra you know me as the arhat the present Buddha, and have comprehended my mind, actions, wisdom, and way of life and release in the way I have mentioned?

Not even that.

You see then Sariputra you do not know the hearts of the arhats, of Buddhas, of past and of the future. Why then do you speak so grandly and so boldly? Why burst forth into such a paean of ecstasy?

What is the meaning of Bodhidharma's coming to China?
The oak tree in the garden

   Joshu

Sermon on the Mount

Blessed are the poor in spirit, for theirs is the kingdom of heaven.

Blessed are they that mourn, for they shall be comforted.

Blessed are the gentle, for they shall inherit the earth.

Blessed are they that hunger and thirst after righteousness, for they shall be filled.

Blessed are the merciful, for they shall obtain mercy.

Blessed are the pure in heart, for they shall see God.

Blessed are the peacemakers, for they shall be called the children of God.

Blessed are they who are persecuted for righteousness' sake, for theirs is the kingdom of heaven.

Blessed are ye, when men shall revile you and persecute you and shall say all manner of evil against you falsely for my sake.

The earth laughs in Flowers -
Ralph Waldo Emerson

On awakening

If one is truly awakened and has realized the fundamental, and he is aware of it himself, in such a case he is actually no longer tied to the poles of practice. But normally, even though the original mind has been awakened through practice so that one is instantaneously awakened to knowing, yet the inertia of habit still lingers. This habit has been formed since the beginning of time, and cannot be completely banished in one go. One must therefore be taught to cut off completely the stream of one's habitual ideas and views that are held in place by unresolved karma. This process of purification is practice. I don't say that one must follow a hard and fast method. One need only be taught the general direction that this

What you hear must first be accepted by your reason; and when your rational mind is deepened and made subtle in an ineffable way, purific your mind will of its own become spontaneously understanding and bright, never to fall back into a state of doubt and confusion.

However numerous and various the subtle teachings are, you will know intuitively how to apply them — which to hold back and which to use — according to the needs of the occasion. ation must take.

Only in this way will you be qualified to sit in the chair and wear your robe as a master of the true art of living.

To sum up, it is of utmost importance to know that Ultimate Reality, the foundation of pure knowing, does not admit of a single speck of dust, but nevertheless in the innumerable paths of action, not a single law is to be broken or thing is to be abandoned. When you can break through with a single stroke of the sword without much ado, then all discrimination between sacred and the profane are annihilated once and for all, and your whole being will reveal true eternity in which reigns the Non-duality of One knowing and the myriad particular things.

Zen Master Issa

What is awakening?

Dogen : My eyes are horizontal; my nose is vertical.

Rumi

Be courageous and discipline yourself

Work. Keep digging your well.
Don't think about getting off from work.
Water is there somewhere.
Submit to a daily practice.
Your loyalty to that is a ring on the door.
Keep knocking, and the joy inside
Will eventually open a window
And look out to see who's there.
Keep working. Exert yourself toward the pull of
God.
Laziness and disdain are not devotions,
Your efforts will bring a result.
You'll watch the wings of divine attraction
Lift from the nest and come toward you!
As dawn lightens, blow out the candle.
Dawn is in your eyes now.
New organs of perceptions come into being as
the result of necessity.
Therefore increase your necessity, so that you
may increase your perception.

"On his death bed my uncle tried to sell me his watch."

Anon

Mullah sells ladders

Mullah coveted his neighbor's pears. Seeing them hanging red and plump made his mouth water. Finally, he could stand it no longer, and he resolved to sample a few of them. Getting a ladder, Mullah propped it up against the wall of the orchard, climbed it, pulled the ladder up after him, and slowly, carefully, lowered the ladder onto the neighbor's side of the wall. Arriving there, he turned ready to get the prize he had come for … and in so doing collided with his neighbor.

"What do you think you are doing?" demanded the neighbor.

"Selling ladders!" retorted Mullah.

"Don't be a fool, you can't sell ladders here," responded the neighbor.

"Its you that is the fool," went on Mullah, "you can sell ladders anywhere."

What does it matter if the grass does not grow, as long as it is green?

> *Gudjief*

The tenth person

Ten people had to cross a river swollen by floods. The crossing was very precarious. After they had crossed, they decided to count their number to confirm all had made the crossing. One of them stepped forward and counted: 1-2-3-4-5-6-7-8-9. There were only nine! Another stepped forward, counted. . . . . . . there were only nine. They were all bewailing the loss of one of their group, when a stranger came along and asked them what the problem was. They said, 'There were ten of us on the other side of the river and now, after a difficult crossing, there are only nine. We have lost one of our friends." The stranger said, "Let me count." So he counted, 1-2-3-4-5-6-7-8-9-10. They were so relieved that they continued their way rejoicing.

However, the stranger too was wrong.

Q: The one who has entered 'the realm of truth' does he still know existence?

Joshu: Who has entered "the realm of truth?"

Q: If that is so then the one who has entered the realm of truth does not know how to leave it?

Joshu: It is not cold ashes. It is not a dead tree. It is a hundred flowers in colorful bloom.

Q: So this then is the state of having entered into the realm of truth?

Joshu: There is no connection.

A cup of tea

It was breakfast time in the trenches on the Western Front. A group of British Tommies was, naturally, brewing tea. Just as the tea was being served, a German patrol, with bayonets drawn, burst in on the group. A Tommy, driven back with a bayonet at his throat, in a moment of panic, held out his tea and offered it to the German. The German turned and fled.

To slice through Buddhas, and Patriarchs
I grip my polished sword.
One glance at my mastery,
The void bites its tusks!
        Daito

God's dog

Robert Louis Stevenson was out walking one day when he came across a man abusing a dog. Stevenson ran across the road towards the man calling out, "Stop that! Stop beating that dog!" The man turned around and growled, "Beat it! This is my dog, and I will deal with it as I please!" "Its God's dog," shouted Stevenson in reply, "and I am here to protect it!"

She walks into the lake without making a ripple.

She moves through the forest without disturbing a blade of grass

He loves melons

A story is told of a Chinese emperor who dispatched a messenger to find a renowned Zen Master. The messenger searched far and wide, and finally came to a village where his questions were no longer received with a blank stare and shake of the head, but with a nod and a smile.

"Yes, I have heard something about a Zen Master living around here. I think you'll find him under the bridge with the beggars."

"Under the bridge with the beggars!?" gasped the messenger. "How will I recognize him?"

"Oh, that is easy. Take a melon with you, he loves melons"

Q. I have heard that men of old said, "It is void, it is clear, it shines of itself." To shine of itself what does that mean?

Joshu.It does not mean that something else shines.

Q. When it fails to shine what then?

Joshu. You have betrayed yourself.

The king and the corpse[4]

Zen master Kyogen said, "It is like a man up a tree hanging from a branch with his mouth; his hands can't grasp a bough, his feet won't reach one. Under the tree there is another man, who asks him the meaning of Daruma's coming from the West. If he doesn't answer, he evades his duty. If he answers, he will lose his life.

    Mumonkan

For ten years every day, a holy man dressed as a beggar would offer the king a fruit. The king accepted the gift and simply passed it back to his treasurer, standing behind him. Without any further ado the beggar would withdraw, and vanish into the crowd of petitioners showing no sign of impatience or disappointment.

One day, after ten years had elapsed a tame monkey, who had escaped from elsewhere in the household, came bounding in, and sat on the arm of the throne. At that moment, the beggar was handing the king his gift of fruit. Playfully, the king passed the fruit to the monkey, who bit into it, and as it did so, a precious jewel fell out of the fruit and rolled onto the floor.

The king turned to the treasurer and asked him, "What has happened to all of the other gifts that this man has brought?" The treasurer did not know how to answer because all that he had done had been to toss the fruit through an open window into the treasure house. So he hastened there and found on the floor a mess of rotten fruit amidst which was a heap of priceless gems.

The king gave the gems to the treasurer, he was not much interested in wealth. His curiosity was, however, peeked, and so when the beggar came the next day the king told him that he could not accept the gift unless the beggar were prepared to stay awhile and talk.

The beggar asked for a private interview, which the king granted, and the beggar was able at last to present his request. He said that he was in search of a hero, a man of great courage to help in a magic enterprise. The king, being interested, asked the holy man to continue. 'The weapons of true heroes,' explained the holy man, 'are renowned in the annals of magic for their exorcising power.' The stranger then asked the king if he would come to the burying ground where the dead of the city were cremated and the criminals hanged.

The king, undaunted, agreed.

On the appointed night, the night of the new moon, the king arrived, alone, girded with a sword, and wearing a dark cloak. As he came to the dreadful burial ground, he became aware of the noise of the ghosts, ghouls and demons, hovering over the uncanny place. As he entered into the light thrown by the funeral pyres he half saw, half divined, the charred of the dead, their blackened bones and crushed skulls scattered around. He was deafened by the shrieks and groans that filled the air.

He went to the appointed rendezvous, where he found his sorcerer inscribing a magic circle on the ground. He was told, "Go to the end of the burial ground and you will find there a corpse; cut it down and bring it here."

The king went to the end of the burial ground as he was bid, and, braving the shrieks and howls of the demons, cut down the corpse, which, as it fell, emitted a mocking groan. The king, thinking it must still be alive, started to inspect it more closely. As he did so a shrill laugh burst out from the corpse, and the king realized that a ghost inhabited it.

"What is funny?" asked the king. The moment he spoke the corpse flew back to the tree.

The king cut the corpse down once more and, this time without a word, mounted it over his shoulder, and proceeded to return to where he had started On the way, the corpse suggested he lighten the king's way by telling a story. The king said not a word.

"Once upon a time a prince went with a hunting party accompanied by a young friend. They went off on their own and, after a while, came upon a beautiful girl bathing on the further shore of a lake they were skirting. The prince saw the girl, who, unobserved by her companions, was making signs, which the prince could not understand. His friend, however, was able to decipher the message, which gave her name, where she lived, and also announced at the same time her love for the prince.

Another day, again on the pretext of going hunting, the two went to the town from which the girl had come. They found lodging in a house owned by an old woman, whom they bribed to be their messenger. The girl sent back a message written in such a way that the woman was unable to understand what it meant. Included in the note was a description of how the prince might find his way to the garden of her house. However, the prince again was unable to understand the message, and gave it to his friend, who was able to read to the prince what it said. The prince followed the instructions, and soon the lovers were able to meet. When the girl learned that it was the friend, and not the prince who had been able to translate all her messages, she was afraid that their rendezvous would be betrayed and resolved to poison the friend.

This man, however, was a match for the princess, and realizing what she was likely to do, devised a plan to teach the girl that he knew how to look after himself, as well as how to protect the prince. He disguised himself as an ascetic, persuaded the princess to play the role of his student, and then brought the girl into suspicion as a witch. He accused her of being the cause of the death of the king's baby son. The princess was condemned to death, by being bound and left naked outside the city walls, exposed to the wild beasts. However, as soon as she was left alone, the prince and his friend snatched her up and carried her off to the prince's realm, where she became his wife and future queen. The princess's parents, only knowing that their daughter had been condemned to death, were so upset at this, that their hearts broke and they died.

"Now who was guilty of the death of the parents? If you know the answer and do not reply your head will explode into a hundred pieces," asked the corpse.

The king felt he knew but realized that if he spoke the corpse would fly back to the tree, but he also feared that if he did not speak his head would explode.

"Neither the prince nor princess were guilty," he declared, "because they were under the spell of love. Nor was the friend guilty, because he too acted out of love for his friend. It was the king of the country, who let things get out of hand, who was to blame." When the last word of the king's judgment was spoken, the corpse groaning in mock agony, flew back to the tree. The king, trudged back, cut down the corpse, and shouldered his burden once more.

Again, the corpse proposed that he lighten the king's travail by telling another story. This concerned three young Brahmins who had lived for a number of years in the home of their spiritual teacher, and all three had fallen in love with his daughter. He was reluctant to bestow her hand on any of the three because by doing so he would cause too much pain for the other two.

But then the girl suddenly fell sick and died. The three young men, stricken by grief, committed her body to the funeral pyre. When the body had been cremated, the first of the students decided to mourn her death by wandering through the world as a beggar ascetic. The second gathered the girl's bones from among the ashes, and took them to a sanctuary alongside the Ganges. The third constructed a hermit's hut over the ashes at the site of the cremation.

On his journeys, the first was a witness to an extraordinary event. He saw a man read a magic charm from a book, and a child, who already had been cremated, was restored to life. Stealing the book, he hurried back to the cremation scene, and arrived just as the one who had gone to the Ganges was dipping the bones in the life-giving stream. The skeleton was reassembled among the ashes. Then the charm was read, and the miracle happened. The girl arose again, more beautiful than ever. But then rivalry sprang up among the three once more, and each claimed the right to her.

"And so to whom does she belong? If you know the answer and do not respond your head will explode," cackled the corpse. The king believed he knew, and was forced to respond. "The one who brought her back to life was performing the duty of the father; the one who looked after her bones fulfilled the duty of the son. But the one who slept on her ashes and did not leave her must be termed her spouse." It was a wise enough judgment — yet the moment it was given the corpse was gone.

Doggedly, the king cut down the corpse once more, and once more trudged on his journey. The voice resumed, and the king was given another riddle, and again, after he had answered, was compelled to retrace his steps. And so it went on, time after time after time, the unrelenting specter in the corpse spun a tale of twisted destinies and tangled lives, while the king was driven to and fro. All of life with its joys and horrors was related in the riddles. And the threads of the fantasies always twisted into knots of right and wrong, tangles of ambiguities and dilemmas.

A story was told for example of the posthumous son of a thief who was faced by a delicate situation when he went to make an offering to his father at a sacred well. His grandmother had been made a widow when she was quite young. Because her relatives had cheated her out of her inheritance, she had to take to the road with her only daughter. On the night of her departure from the village, she happened upon a thief who had been impaled upon a stake, and was just about to die. In terrible agony, scarcely able to breath, he asked if he could marry the little girl. He asked this so that he would have prior call on her son, when later in life she had one, who would then be obliged to make offerings due to the soul of a deceased father. In return he would tell the woman where she could find hidden treasure.

The marriage was concluded in an informal but binding way, and the thief died. The mother and daughter became heirs to a considerable fortune. When she grew older the girl fell in love with a young Brahmin, and he consented to be her lover but at a price, because there was a courtesan he wanted to pay. The young woman conceived a son and, following the instructions of a dream that she had shortly after the birth, deposited the babe with a thousand pieces of gold at the entrance of the palace of a certain king. As it happened, the king, who had no son, dreamed that same night that a son would be deposited at his door and, taking the dream for a sign, brought the young child up as is own son.

Many years later, after the king had died, the prince, heir to the throne, went to make an offering to his departed father. He went to the holy well where the dead were accustomed to stretch forth their hands to receive the proffered gifts. But instead of a single hand reaching out, three hands were stretched out: that of the thief, that of the Brahmin and that of the king. The prince did not know what to do. Even the priests attending the offering did not know. "Well," challenged the corpse, "into which hand should he deposit his offering?"

Again threatened with the explosion of his skull, the king pronounced a judgment, "The thief should get the offering. The Brahmin," he said, "sold himself, the king was paid by the gold pieces left with the child, but the thief had paid both for the begetting and the fosterage." Off went the corpse back to the tree.

When will it all end? In all twenty–four riddles were posed, and the king had to announce an answer to them all, and suffer the consequences of this announcement, except the last one.

A father and son, members of a tribe of huntsmen, were on a hunting expedition when they happened to come upon the footprints of two women. The father was a widower, and the son not yet married. The practiced eyes of the huntsmen saw that a noble woman and her daughter, fugitives of some aristocratic house, had left the prints. The larger prints suggested the beauty of a queen, and the smaller ones the beauty of a princess. The son was quite excited, and after some considerable discussion, finally persuaded the father that they should go after the women. The father should marry the one with the larger footprints, and the son would marry the one with the smaller prints, and the two took a solemn oath that this is what they would do.

They went on the trail in great haste, and finally came upon the two unhappy women. Just as the huntsmen had suspected, they were in anxious flight from a situation that had developed at home where the king had unexpectedly died. There was, however, a problem: the daughter had left the larger footprints, and the mother the smaller. According to their oath, therefore, the son would have to marry the queen and the father the princess.

They were married, and the four returned to the home of the men. Then the women conceived. "Tell me just how were the two sons, who were born as a consequence, related to each other?" asked the corpse.

The king carrying his burden was unable to find any unequivocal term for their relationship. An enigma had been found which could strike him dumb. And so he walked along, bemusing the problem in silence: the boys would be living ambiguities.

But is it not always so—with all things—in some respect? Is not everything in some deep way, its own opposite? Even though the discriminating mind with its logic, categories of language, and thought may refuse to accept the ambiguity, nevertheless every feature, every moment of life, includes somehow, qualities diametrically opposed to those apparently implied.

"All true good carries with it conditions that are contradictory, and as a consequence is impossible. He, who keeps his attention really fixed on this impossibility, and acts, will do what is good... In the same way all truth contains a contradiction." Simone Weil, an anthology (Virago; London) 1986.

At sea

O voyagers, O seamen,
You who come to port, and you whose bodies
Will suffer the trial and judgment of the sea,
Or whatever event, this is your real destination
So Krishna, as when he admonished Arjuna
On the field of battle,
Not fare well
  But fare forward, voyagers.

T.S. Eliot

You are at sea. The boat you are in is small, can scarcely carry one person with just a few provisions. The night is dark, neither stars nor moon relieve the gloom. You are lost. You do not know where land is, whether it is near, or a thousand miles away. The wind is rising, gusting and the waves get higher, white crested and, I forgot to mention it, the boat has a leak. Not a really serious one, you can bale it out, provided, that is, you keep on baling. By turns you feel hopeful then despairing, anxious then cocky, afraid then bold, panicky then angry, angry at yourself for ever having got into the boat, at the guy who made the boat, at the stupid sea, at anything, anything and everything. You keep wishing things were different, that the boat was bigger, that it didn't leak, that you were near land. Then you forget to bale, and the thing begins to founder, and in a sweat and fury you bale and bale until after a while things settle down. Or at least they're not quite as bad as they were.

It is cold and the wind gets stronger, now the waves wash over the side — not much, just a little now and again. But will it get worse? Will you be able to bale enough? What will happen if, if, if... Thunder rumbles, you wonder, wonder what next? Can things get worse? You are so desperate, tears spring to your eyes; if only, if only...Ceaselessly, you search into the darkness, but all you see is more darkness, opaque, impenetrable, menacing. What there is to see, what it is you are looking for, where to look for it, how to recognize it if you see it, you don't know. But you do know you must keep searching, searching, searching.

And then you see a light. It is definitely a light. There it is! It is a light. It is small, in fact, lets face it, so tiny, and it seems so far away, that it almost seems a mirage. But no: doubt is not possible; it is **REAL.** Relief washes over you: just pure joy. A light means land. Not only is there really land: but it is right there and reachable. Not only is it reachable, but also the light shows the precise direction to go. Mark you, your situation hasn't changed, the boat is still as small, it leaks just as much, the sea is still as rough, the night is just as dark. Indeed in your moment of relief you've forgotten to bale and the boat is foundering! Quickly get the baler and start to work! But even so the light shines.

Just keep going now, never mind about the fear and the hopes, the fear that there is no land, that you'll never find a direction, that it will be too far, that fate is against you. Even as all these fears rise up they melt away in the reality of the light. The hope that when you see land it will be made of milk and honey, that you don't have to go to the land, but simply have to wait for the land to come to you, the hope that one day you'll wake up and find the sea has turned into land, that there'll be some wonderful reward for all the fears and labor, that you are the first, the best, the most intrepid of explorers, all these irrational fears and hopes, daydreams, speculations and wishes rise up and melt away in the reality of the light.

If someone were to challenge you and say that it is not really a light that you are seeing, you would laugh, and go on your way. Now you know the light that the sea threw up with its phosphorescence, that the imagination threw up in its terror and despair, that the intellect threw up in its futile attempt to regain mastery of the situation, all these were just phantoms, phantoms of the past. The light is a sure beacon and nothing can make you afraid of the dark and gloom again.

Its something like the words of the old Christian hymn:

> Lead kindly light amid the encircling gloom,
> Lead thou me on.
> The night is dark and I am far from home,
> Lead thou me on.
> Guide thou my feet.
> I do not ask to see the distant scene,
> One step enough for me

But still there is work. But, as you work, you see yet another light, and yet another, then a shape looms up and another. These do not have the same impact that the first sighting of light had, they do not give the same utter relief from an intolerable burden of doubt and dismay, except perhaps when what you had thought to be a distant mountain turns out to be the roof of a warehouse; not miles and miles away but almost within hailing distance. Each new light, each new shape is but confirmation making deeper, more natural and inevitable the original awakening. There is now a deep security in the awareness that you will reach land, that you will walk. Then even the possibility of foundering, and therefore the need to bale, will be no more.

But now you must work without haste and fully committed to doing the work. You know that a certain distance must be covered, that a certain amount of water has to be baled, that prayers, pleas, magic or miracles will not take away the need for labor. Without dreams — these would just interfere; without expectation — what is there to expect; without hopes — these would be hopes for the wrong thing, one just goes on working.

Free like a white cloud what is it like? It does not compare with the spring breeze that gently touches everything

Joshu

And now we are saved absolutely, we need not say from what, we are at home in the universe, and in principle, and in the main, feeble and timid creatures as we are, there is nothing within the world or without that can make us afraid.

Bosanquet

And all shall be well and
All manner of thing shall be well
When the tongues of flame are in-folded
Into the crowned knot of fire
And the fire and the rose are one.

T.S.Eliot

Notes

[1] Jaksa James A. and Stech Ernest L. *Voices from the Silence*. Toronto: Griffin House 1980 page 40.

[2] Luke 15:11-32 (New International Version, ©2010)

[3] Adapted from the last Chapter ON HUMILITY in the *Supreme Doctrine* by Hubert Benoit.

[4] This story is an adaptation of part of an ancient tale told by Heinrich Zimmer in his book *The King and the Corpse. (1960) (Meridian Books, inc. New York.)*

www.ingramcontent.com/pod-product-compliance
Lightning Source LLC
Chambersburg PA
CBHW071546040426
42452CB00008B/1095